THINGS REVEALED

BELONG TO US

PAIGE JACKSON

All scripture used is New King James Version (NKJV) unless otherwise noted at the location of the quote.

The Holy Bible, New King James Version Copyright © 1982 by Thomas Nelson, Inc.

Holy Bible, New International Version®, NIV® Copyright © 1973, 1978, 1984, 2011 by Biblica, Inc.® Used by permission. All rights reserved worldwide.

American Standard Version (ASV) © 1901 by Public Domain

King James Version (KJV) Public Domain

Amplified Bible (AMP) © 1954, 1958, 1962, 1964, 1965, 1987 by The Lockman Foundation

Cover Art: Paige Jackson
Cover Design: Elizabeth Little, http://hyliian.deviantart.com
Interior Book Design: Ellen Sallas, The Author's Mentor,
    www.LittleRoniPublishers.com

ISBN-13: 978-1497412972

ISBN-10: 1497412978

Also available in eBook

PRINTED IN THE UNITED STATES OF AMERICA

Endorsements

Writing on the conviction that "God's Word is always God's Will," Paige Jackson has given us a practical and powerful tool for successful intercession. Truly born out of her own life challenges, pain, and her life's heart-cries, Paige gives us insight on how to pray effectively, using the Word of God for all of life's challenges.

Whether for healing, marriage, children, the grace to forgive, or intense spiritual warfare, Paige shows us the power of declaring God's promises through prayer, and reminding ourselves through these declarations that He is at work to bring His word to pass in our circumstances.

I highly recommend this Godly intercessor's book to all who long to join the heart of Him Who "ever lives to make Intercession."

~Steve Franklin
Bishop/Pastor
Covenant Heirs Int'l/Steve Franklin Ministries

In *Things Revealed Belong to Us*, Paige Jackson writes of things that were given to her by God that changed her life and circumstances. You, dear reader, now have the opportunity to learn of those things from the pages of this book. This is a must-read for anyone who wants to know those things that God reveals for the life He intends us to live. Don't miss this message!

~Phyllis H. Hendry,
President & CEO
Lead Like Jesus.com

DEDICATION

I want to give thanks and praise to my heavenly Father, Jesus, and the Holy Spirit. They have truly been my strength, my song, and very present help in trouble.

I want to bless and thank my husband, David, who has stood with me, prayed with me and for me as I learned to become an overcomer.

I thank my sons, Corey and Brice, for letting me tell part of their stories, so people who read them can be set free. I also thank their wives and my grandchildren. They are the greatest gift God has given me on this earth.

With all my heart I thank my friends who have prayed for me and my family for years, and have given me the privilege of praying for theirs. Thank you for your lifelong encouragement (some over 25 years). I love you all dearly. These women know how to go before God's throne and pray until situations change. Bless you!!

I also express my deepest love and gratitude to my sweet friends and pastors, Jon and Lisa Potter. Their love is limitless, even to people they have just met. They have been a great encouragement to me. They both have the heart of a revivalist and want to see the world changed so we can live in unity and be one, as Jesus said that He and the Father are one. I am so thrilled I get to walk with them in this time.

TABLE OF CONTENTS

FOREWORD

If you're like me, when you really need know something, you jump on Google as the path of least resistance to the information you want. If you really need access to that kind of data on a regular basis, you hit the app store to ensure that what you need is instantly available via your smart phone or iPad. We love these tools because they're convenient and sometimes critical shortcuts to what keeps the business of life running smoothly.

For thousands of years, the treasure of God's word was passed down through oral tradition. Not only was it written, it was also given by those who had experienced its authenticity in serving and hearing the voice of the One who was the Author and Finisher of their faith. In our high-tech world, there are now scores of places where you can get instant access to The Word of God. These are wonderful, but I am at a place in my life that I want to surround myself with those who yes, know the Word; but far more importantly, I want to know people who have engaged in a lifestyle of intimate encounters with the God of the Word!

For 20+ years, Paige Jackson has been far more than a friend to me and our family; Paige has been a "watchman" on the spiritual walls of our lives and over our children. Out of her own crucible of an incurable physical disease, she tediously pushed through great adversity daily to mine out the treasury of God's truths. With this work, Things Revealed Belong to Us, Paige describes and demonstrates how weaving these truths and their application in prayer, forever transformed her marriage, her children, and generations to come. This work is a not only a chronicle of what she and God did together, but even more, an easy "how to" manual for the same principles that God gave her, to alter the trajectory of your life in ways you couldn't imagine!

It has been said that "an argument is no match for an experience." With candor, humor, and even some tears, Paige offers us the incredible privilege to "pull up a chair and have a cup of coffee," as she recalls her experience that has trumped every argument that Hell has assaulted her with to nullify her faith. Friends, I want to assure you that Paige Jackson knows God and knows His voice! I have learned thus far in life, that you and I can acquire wisdom through a mess or through a mentor. The latter path is always God's highest and best!

For every young believer, and especially every young mother, you will find this book a tool, a weapon, and even a "friend," that complements the light of God's word in helping you to navigate everything you face; from the little challenges of life, to traversing through those long dark nights of the soul!

As her pastor and friend, I unreservedly recommend that you read this book and keep it close to your night stand. It is a template on how you too can begin to document the power of knowing, hearing, speaking and standing on God's infallible word!

Jonathan S. Potter
Pastor, Canvas Church, Birmingham AL
Author - Spiritual Identity Fraud
       "Restoring God's Sons and Daughters"

INTRODUCTION

I am just a normal mother and wife. Years ago, when I learned God wanted me to live and not die and I could raise my two boys, I was changed forever. Wouldn't you be?

The Word of God became so real to me, it was almost tangible. I realized I was on a journey with God to know Him, to grow deeper in faith, to believe for the impossible. I was to see the things I had not known before.

The Bible says we will do great exploits (Daniel 11:32) and that's what I thought I was going to do, and I still do. I want the lost saved. I want to see revival in our time. I thought I was pouring over the Bible day and night, reading everything I could about miracles and faith, so I could stand as an overcomer, and I was, but I also came through all that for you, dear reader.

Every trial, everything I learned in my last 30 years has been for me, but also for you. You were on God's heart all along.

I believe God knew that one day I'd write all these experiences down, in order to help you in your deepest, darkest hours. I wish I'd kept notes, but when I went through suffering, I didn't want to record it. I didn't even think of it. As years went by, I realized we all struggle. And some people's paths are harder than others'.

I believe what I have learned and now written in this book will change you, your family, your friends. I pray you will be "enlightened by His Spirit" as you read, so your faith will rise and you will learn to be an overcomer in every area of your life too. It is possible!

~ Paige Jackson

We overcome "by the Blood of the Lamb
and the Word of (our) testimony." *Revelation 12:11*

Deuteronomy 29:29

The secret *things belong* to the L<small>ORD</small> our
God, but those *things which are* revealed
belong to us and to our children forever, that
we may do all the words of this law.

1

WILL HE FIND FAITH ON THE EARTH?

At age 30, my normal way of living was about to change. I was thrown into a personal hurricane. It's hard to build a house in a hurricane. It is too wet to pour a foundation and too dark to build a structure.

But that's exactly what I had to do. I had no tools to face this crisis. That's how most crises are. They come without warning. No one could help me, not even doctors.

A friend of mine framed and gave me this scripture years ago. She said, "God told me to provoke you with this scripture and to tell you to provoke and teach others, so they won't be found lacking when He comes."

> **Luke 18:7-8 KJV** And shall not God avenge his own elect, which cry day and night unto him, though he bear long with them? [8] I tell you that he will avenge them speedily. Nevertheless when the Son of man cometh, **shall he find faith on the earth**?

My friend used the word *provoke* which means to excite or stimulate to action, especially to bring about or to call forth. She said, "God has commissioned you concerning faith." When she told me this I knew in the deepest part of me it was true. Talking to people about faith, believing God's Word and acting like it is true is my passion. People say find your passion in life and pursue it with all your heart. My passion for years has been to encourage people to believe God's Word, pray His Word back to Him over every circumstance in their lives, and watch what the God of the Universe will do.

The Bible says, "Without faith it is impossible to please Him" (Hebrews 11:6a), and that He "uphold(s) all things by the Word of His power" (Heb 1:3).

I can say and believe this now, knowing that all this is true, because I learned it in places in my life where my mind and heart were plagued with fear. Some people call this place "the dark night of the soul." I didn't know that phrase during the dark days of my life. I only knew I needed help. I knew "my help come(s) from the Lord" (Psalm 121:2), but I did not see Him, feel Him or hear Him.

I was 30 years old. I was going to church, teaching children's church and going to Bible studies. I loved God with all my heart. I had been in church most of my life. I was saved at 14 years old. I felt I had always loved Jesus when I walked that aisle and told the man down front I wanted to be saved. The man gave me a card to fill out about becoming a member of the church. I left that day feeling a little confused and empty on the inside, but eventually someone explained the gospel to me. Jesus took all my sins from me and they were nailed with Him on the cross; He died for me there and was raised back to life on the third day. If I believed that, then I was a Christian. So I did believe it, and confessed that I was a Christian.

I lived what looked like a normal Christian life. We went

to church every Sunday after we married. We taught our children Bible stories and Christian songs. We were excited about our faith and went to a great evangelistic church. People were getting saved every Sunday.

I felt like I was in a dark pit, absolutely alone.

I wish I could say I pulled up my spiritual loins (I Peter 1:13) and fought a good fight, but I didn't. Not at first. I didn't feel God. I was crying out desperate prayers, but I wasn't hearing His voice. Oh, I know He was speaking, but the loud blast of fear around me drowned out any sound of hope.

I thought no one understood how I felt. How could they? They were all going about their lives and I was lying in a bed filled with self-pity. Knowing myself, I probably even felt pretty justified in my self-pity.

People were gracious and brought us food. They said they were praying for me. But I didn't hear any prayers out loud. My husband, David, was numb. What can a man do when he has a wife that's bed-ridden, in pain, with no answers from the doctors, and two little boys to take care of? He was in his own pit of self-pity and confusion. His hurricane was different, but still devastating. He threw desperate prayers to heaven.

My Personal Hurricane

David and I had been married for eight years. Our marriage had been pretty rocky. We were both dedicated Christians. We looked good on the outside, but we were far from good. We went to church with our two boys. Corey, the oldest, was four, and Brice was eight months.

It was the end of March 1980. I had put on a little baby weight from pregnancy and had a hard time losing it. One day, I decided to try playing tennis with a friend. I had played a lot in college, but hadn't picked up a racket in years. When I looked in the mirror, I felt I looked more like a dough boy than an hourglass. It was discouraging. Having always been thin, it was exciting to get back on the court.

Tennis went okay, but over the next few days my feet became really sore. I could barely walk. Then little red dots speckled my heels. Every step I took brought excruciating pain. I hobbled around for a week and could hardly put my feet on the floor. I thought I had overdone it with the tennis outing since I was really out of shape.

David finally said, "You're going to have to go to the doctor." So we found an internist someone recommended. He told me I had tendonitis. He was the doctor, of course I believed him. He put me on a drug called Butazolidin Alka. After a month on this drug, there were no improvements, so I took myself off it.

The reason I remember the name of the drug so vividly is because about a year later I was reading the newspaper. There was an article on drugs that caused deaths that had been taken off the market. There in bold black letters was the drug I had taken for a month with no side effects. The Lord had preserved my life, but there were still no answers to my problem.

I read a quote from Corrie Ten Boom once that I love: "There is no pit so deep, that God's love is not deeper still." I do love that quote! But it is a whole lot easier after you get out of your physical or spiritual hurricane to really believe it is true.

Growing up in Florida, I survived several hurricanes. A hurricane's wind can be so strong it blows houses off their foundations. Its winds can erode sand in a few hours, washing away beaches. Hurricanes can turn a bright sunny day dark in a matter of hours. The middle of the hurricane is an eye. At 10 years old I stood on my front porch in the eye of a hurricane. It was pitch black, silent, no wind. Then we ran into the house and shut the door. The calm was over and the storm beat against the house again, leaving behind high flood waters. But we were safe.

During these months of sickness, pain, rushes of emotion, words being spoken around me like I wasn't there, and hopelessness swirled around me. Yet I was in the secret place. As David wrote in Psalm 91, I was "sheltered under God's wing." I wish I had *felt* the comfort of His wings, but even though I didn't, I was about to learn His Word is true.

The knots on my feet began to appear on my knees. They looked like huge inflamed boils. My joints, knees, elbows, wrists and thumbs, starting hurting. I couldn't push myself up off the bed in the morning or off the sofa. I kept going to doctors. They were baffled with all the symptoms.

What bothered me more was not just experiencing the physical pain, but dealing with the emotional pain of not being able to care for my boys. My mom came to live with us. She was great, but I hated lying around or sitting there all the time, watching her work around the house, cooking and playing with the boys. One morning when Brice was crying in his crib, I couldn't pick him up. My mom got him and fed him breakfast. I called out to God a lot, "What is wrong with me? Help me!" God is our "very present help in trouble" (Psalm 46:1b). I was in trouble.

David knew I was sick, but not how sick, until I was in bed all the time and he had to carry me to the bathroom. I think he thought, *Well, she'll just get over this.* Sometimes it is hard to relate to someone else's pain, especially long term. The burden that sickness puts on others is like water being sucked through a straw. The water goes slowly and the glass becomes empty. After a while, the family or caregivers get weary, almost lethargic, in their duties. Oh, they love the person, but their lives are being stolen too. Nothing is normal.

The Thief Comes to Steal

> **John 10:10** (AMP) The thief comes only in order to steal and kill and destroy. I came that they may have *and* enjoy life, and have it in abundance.

This pertains to salvation, but it also describes the tactics of the enemy in our lives, such as sickness, deception, poverty, etc.

One day a distant family member called me, I thought, to see how I was doing. She said, "I know your mom is there, but you can't expect her to give up her whole life to take care of you. You don't know how long this will be. You need to find other help." Well, that was another blow on top of everything else I was experiencing.

We couldn't afford to pay for help. David had to work. It took me a while to forgive her, but I knew she was right. Everyone's lives were being stolen from.

My pit kept getting deeper.

One day David thought of a high school friend who worked at a hospital. He called and asked him if he could pull some strings and get me in to see a doctor at the Rheumatology clinic. The wait was at least a month. I needed to see a rheumatologist immediately. So, through David's friend Tom, God worked a miracle. I got in the next week.

I was really excited because these doctors were specialists. I thought *now, finally, surely, these doctors can find out what's wrong with me!*

However, I was about to find out that even when doctors diagnose the problem, it doesn't mean it is over. As one of my teachers says—But God!—God was about to do a miracle in me that would change my life and family forever!

Psalm 46:10

Be still and know that I am God.

2

THE DIAGNOSIS

The rheumatologist pressed on one inflamed knot after another. I can only guess he had no idea how painful they were. I could hardly bear the exam. They did lung x-rays. The doctor suggested that I have part of one of the knots removed and tested, intimating that it could be cancer. Everything in me screamed, "This is not cancer!" But I let them take a long metal tool, with a hollow place at one end and screw it into the lower part of my leg. When they removed it, it had a plug of skin stuck in it. They put the plug in a bottle to send it off, then put a dot band-aid on the hole in my leg.

They asked me lots of questions. The doctor was very matter-of-fact and had no bedside manner. A young intern assisted him who seemed to really care and was anxious to help. They did lots of blood tests and other tests. They were pretty sure I had rheumatoid arthritis, but I wasn't. Nothing added up.

After all that, we had no new information to help us!

They sent me home with a 7-day Prednisone pack. I was adamant about not taking it, because my mom had been on Prednisone 20 years earlier with lots of side effects. But David insisted…it was just a week's worth of medicine.

I took it. I can tell you I felt completely well. Every pain left my body. I couldn't believe it! To be pain free after six to eight weeks was amazing.

At the end of that week, I thought I was really well. I had taken the last pill. The pain at my ankles rose up my legs like floodwaters. It kept rising, all the way to my thumb joints.

"What is this?" I was crying out to the Lord again! Disappointment cloaked me in heaviness.

You Want to Hear People's Prayers

During these weeks of sickness, people I know had been praying for me. My dad came after a couple of weeks, and he would sit on my bed and hold my hand. My dad was a sweet man who loved the Lord.

I said, "Daddy, I want you to pray for me."

"Well, Honey, I do pray for you, all the time," he said.

"I want you to pray for me now."

He looked kind of embarrassed and said, "Honey, I do pray for you."

He could not pray out loud for healing for me. In fact, no one prayed for me aloud. I really needed to hear the prayers. I wanted them spoken out loud, but no one did.

I went back to the doctor the following week. The intern came in to see me first. He said, "Mrs. Jackson, this is kind of embarrassing, but the tissue that was taken out of your leg and sent to the lab has been lost." I couldn't believe it!

I said, "Well, I'm not having another one taken. I know it is not cancer."

He smiled and said, "I don't blame you."

Another week went by and finally it was the intern who discovered the diagnosis. The doctor compared an old lung x-ray with the new one and saw deterioration in my lungs. When they researched it, combined with the knots on my legs (called erythema nodosum), the diagnosis was a rare disease called Sarcoidosis.

They told me that in 1973 doctors found that people who had the lung problems and arthritic symptoms together had this disease. Before that time, doctors would do surgery, splitting the breast bone, to take a piece of the lung to test it. I was glad it hadn't shown up in me until the 1980's!

The doctors took many photos of my legs because they had never seen anyone local with fair skin having this disease. It was common in African Americans and in Scandinavians. But I was not of either lineage. I am Dutch-Irish with maybe a little German. They seemed thrilled to get good photos for their files.

I returned home with very little knowledge of the disease. They said, "We can't do anything about it." The word "terminal" was mentioned. I was in that low, devastated place again. They sent me home with a new drug not even on the market yet, Naproxen. It is similar to Aleve. I was to take three tablets a day to cover the pain, but it was still there. It was like wearing a coat when it is freezing outside. You can feel the cold, but it is not too bad.

Now, I'm sorry to say, I felt more mentally down than ever. My mom was still with us, cleaning, cooking, and taking care of the boys. Friends would still come by with food, and sometimes take Corey home with them to play.

One Sunday, David took the boys to church. I sat in bed and flipped the channels on the television. I had never watched TV on a Sunday morning since I was always in church, so I had no idea what was on or who was preaching.

I can imagine just how excited Jesus must have been watching me there on the edge of all He was about to reveal and teach me. Maybe the angels were jumping up and down seeing His excitement. I have a vivid imagination.

As I flipped through the channels, a loud preaching man I had never seen before was talking rather abruptly. I watched him for a few minutes. I had no idea that one chapter of my life as I had always known it was about to close and a whole new book was about to begin. God was going to enlighten me by His Spirit (Ephesians 1:8).

I thought I was dying, but God was going to teach me to live.

Acts 10:38b

(Jesus) went about doing good and healing all who
were oppressed by the devil,
for God was with Him.

3

God Wants You Well

The preacher I was watching was adamant about his text. My attention was captured by 10 little words I had never heard put together before. I had grown up in church but I'd never heard these words. He said,

"God wants you well and the devil wants you sick."

Everything in me was riveted to the screen. Hope began to bubble up in me. I had never heard such bold preaching. I had never heard a sermon on healing. It was about time!

I got the notebook from beside my bed and wrote down every scripture he said. I wasn't familiar with many of them, even as much as I had read the Bible. I had even been to Bible college for over a year, and I had never seen those verses. I sure hadn't heard any sermons on them.

When the program ended, I looked up every verse. Over the course of a day or two, I wrote out each one, longhand, so I could read them easily, over and over. Hope swelled in me for the first time in months. I had been sick about two and a half months by then.

The diagnosis had not changed, but something had happened in my mind and spirit. I did not share it with my family yet. I was trying to understand it myself. I was beginning to build my spiritual house. A house built on faith. Even though the hurricane was the same, I was different. One man's words speaking truth had opened my eyes to begin to believe the full gospel.

This man said, "Jesus wants you well and the devil wants you sick." I had read all the verses now, studied them, and believed it was the truth!

I had been in bed so long, people seemed unaware about the depth my condition. It is the same as agreeing with what is going on in life if you think there's nothing you can do about it. Thoughts like *If God wanted me well, he would have healed me*, or *If God wanted to save him/her He would*, are just not truth. It is not how God works. It is not Biblical.

Our Part Is to Believe

God is "not willing that any should perish" (II Peter 3:9). He says if we believe that Jesus died on the cross for our personal sins and that He was raised from the dead in three days, and then we confess it before men, we are saved. Then according to the Word we will live with Him for eternity (John 3:15). Our part is to believe.

This preacher was saying the same thing. When we have believed Jesus died for us and we become Christians, one of the benefits of salvation is healing, because Jesus bore the stripes on his back for healing of all diseases.

> **I Peter 2:24** who Himself (Jesus) bore our sins in His own body on the tree, that we, having died to sins, might live for righteousness—by whose stripes you were healed.

20

There it was, right there in the Bible. I had never seen it. I had never been told about it. How could I believe that it was part of God's plan if I didn't know about it?

I had taken for granted, like most Christians do, that sickness came to mankind at the Fall recorded in Genesis, but no one told me that Jesus paid for sin and sickness on the cross. I thought that we just had to bear it; sickness was part of life.

Now I felt my whole brain and spirit being rewired, renewed, to see the Word of God as living. A true living Word. The words not just to become a Christian and get through life as best as we can, but a Word that changes situations in life. And this living Word belonged to me, because Jesus and the Word are one, and Jesus lives in me!

> **John 1:1** In the beginning was the Word, and the Word was with God, and the Word was God.

The Declaration

One Saturday morning, while everyone was still sleeping, I put on my robe, took my list of scriptures, and went out in our backyard. The pain was still there, but I could function because of the Naproxen.

I sat in a lawn chair and looked at the scriptures in my lap. I really didn't plan it out, I just picked up the list, held it up to the sky, and I said, "Lord, I've never seen these scriptures before, but I believe they are true. From today on, I'm going to pray this Word back to you. It is what You say about me and I believe what it says. Lord, I want to live. I want to raise my boys. I'm the best mother they could ever have. So I thank you for healing me in Jesus' name."

Well, there was no lightning that struck, no fire that fell

down to consume the papers. Not even a tiny ray of sun to highlight a particular verse. I stood up and walked back into the house.

I was determined to pray the Word back to God, so that's what I did, day and night. Praying scriptures all day under my breath, I'd help with the housework as much as possible. I still hadn't shared much with my family. I had to get it deep inside me first. The more I spoke the scriptures, the deeper it went into my heart. Which in itself is scriptural:

> **Romans 10:17 (NKJV)** So then faith comes by hearing, and hearing by the word of God.

When I first began to pray God's Word back to Him I would say, "Thank You, Lord, that You bore every sickness for me and carried every disease" (Matthew 8:17 Paige paraphrase). "Thank You that You sent Your Word and healed me" (Psalm 107:20). "Thank You, Lord that Your Word is life to my bones and health to my flesh" (Proverbs 3:8 & 4:22 Paige paraphrase). I was saying it to myself out loud, but not really believing it. I was saying it and praying it, but it was just in my head. I had to get it down into my heart.

His Word Was More Real Than the Pain

After a few weeks the truth of this Word became rooted in me. It was more real than the red knots that I saw or the pain I felt. It's not easy to explain, but the life in the Word pushed every bit of sickness out of my body. I knew I was getting better. The knots on my legs were going away, but whether I saw it or not, would have made no difference. I knew I was healed. I just *knew* it!

I was taking three Naproxen pills a day, so on my own, I decided to take two, then one. One day, I said to myself, "If I can take just one, then I can take none." Then I threw the rest in the trash. I never took another pill (in relation to this disease). Soon all my symptoms were gone. God had performed a miracle for me!

> **Jeremiah 1:12b** for I will hasten my word to perform it.

My energy level was a little low; I had been in bed for most of three months. The doctor called one day and said my breathing tests were low. I needed to come in and be tested again.

"I've been in bed for months," I said, "Would it make a difference if I got up and was a little more active?"

He said, "Well, I guess it would."

Then I replied, "Really, doctor, I believe God has healed me."

He said, "If you need anything, call us." And hung up.

I never spoke to him, or any other doctor there ever again. That was 32 years ago.

About a year later, I was supposed to go on a business trip with David. I developed a deep cough. So before I left on the trip, I went to a different doctor someone recommended. I told the doctor before he did the lung x-rays, that the Lord had healed me of Sarcoidosis. He looked at me a little strangely and left the room.

After the x-ray, he said, "Well, you don't have bronchitis. And the other disease you said you had...you don't have that either."

You know, I really didn't even think about getting a doctor's confirmation of my healing. I already knew it. But God was so good to confirm it to me anyway.

My life was back to normal. My mom went home. I could be a mom again. I cooked, I cleaned, I went to church. I had a new perspective on daily living. I was grateful I could get down on my knees and wipe up spilled apple juice or stand in the kitchen and make a cake or throw a baseball in the yard. I could do the normal things that before had seemed a little mundane.

Life was normal! But I was totally different!

I was walking in a new way of praying and believing. My family and everyone I knew was the same.

Everyone was excited I was healed, but it was hard for me to explain what I had been through. They had seen the physical side of it, but the spiritual side had been just God and me alone.

There were things that caught me by surprise about Christians. I was in a joyous place of revelation, "hungering and thirsting" for more truth (Matthew 5:6). I wondered, *what else have I missed*? It was difficult to express the way I felt. I didn't feel better or smarter than everybody. I was just passionate about walking and living in all that God had done for me. It was a lonely place, and it lasted for several years.

SCRIPTURES TO STAND ON HEALING

The following are the list of Scriptures I used to stand for my healing for your easy reference. I hope you will search out the Word for more.

Proverbs 4:20-22 My son, give attention to my words;
Incline your ear to my sayings. [21] Do not let them depart from your eyes; Keep them in the midst of your heart; [22] For they *are* life to those who find them, And health to all their flesh.

II Corinthians 1:20 For all the promises of God in Him *are* Yes, and in Him Amen, to the glory of God through us.

John 14:13-14 And whatever you ask in My name, that I will do, that the Father may be glorified in the Son. [14] If you ask anything in My name, I will do *it.*

John 15:7 If you abide in Me, and My words abide in you, you will ask what you desire, and it shall be done for you.

Hebrews 11:6 But without faith *it is* impossible to please *Him,* for he who comes to God must believe that He is, and *that* He is a rewarder of those who diligently seek Him.

I John 5:14-15 Now this is the confidence that we have in Him, that if we ask anything according to His will, He hears us. [15] And if we know that He hears us, whatever we ask, we know that we have the petitions that we have asked of Him.

Exodus 15:26c For I *am* the LORD who heals you.

Hebrews 13:8 Jesus Christ *is* the same yesterday, today, and forever.

Matthew 8:17 that it might be fulfilled which was spoken by Isaiah the prophet, saying: "He Himself took our infirmities And bore our sicknesses."

Mark 11:24 Therefore I say to you, whatever things you ask when you pray, believe that you receive *them,* and you will have *them.*

Matthew 18:19 (KJV) Again I say unto you, That if two of you shall agree on earth as touching any thing that they shall ask, it shall be done for them of my Father which is in heaven.

Exodus 23:25 So you shall serve the LORD your God, and He will bless your bread and your water. And I will take sickness away from the midst of you.

Psalm 118:17 I shall not die, but live, And declare the works of the LORD.

Psalm 107:20 He sent His word and healed them,
And delivered *them* from their destructions.

Galatians 3:13-14 Christ has redeemed us from the curse of the law, having become a curse for us (for it is written, "Cursed *is* everyone who hangs on a tree"), [14] that the blessing of Abraham might come upon the Gentiles in Christ Jesus, that we might receive the promise of the Spirit through faith.

III John 1:2 (KJV) Beloved, I wish above all things that thou mayest prosper and be in health, even as thy soul prospereth.

II Timothy 1:7 For God has not given us a spirit of fear, but of power and of love and of a sound mind.

Ephesians 6:10-13 Finally, my brethren, be strong in the Lord and in the power of His might. [11] **Put on the whole armor of God,** that you may be able to stand against the wiles of the devil. [12] For we do not wrestle against flesh and blood, but against principalities, against powers, against the rulers of the darkness of this age, against spiritual *hosts* of wickedness in the heavenly *places.* [13] Therefore take up the whole armor of God, that you may be able to withstand in the evil day, and having done all, to stand.

John 10:10 The thief does not come except to steal, and to kill, and to destroy. I have come that they may have life, and that they may have *it* more abundantly.

Jeremiah 30:17a For I will restore health to you and heal you of your wounds,' says the LORD,

Isaiah 53:5 But He *was* wounded for our transgressions, *He was* bruised for our iniquities; The chastisement for our peace *was* upon Him, And by His stripes we are healed.

Joel 3:10c Let the weak say, 'I *am* strong.'

Hebrews 4:2b

…but the word which they heard did not profit them, not being mixed with faith in those who heard it.

4

Jesus Came to Destroy the Works of the Devil

Everyone we knew was excited that I was well. David was glad, of course. I was whole again and not in pain. The pressure of doing everything was off his shoulders. The only problem now is that he didn't know how to respond to this new woman.

For months I tried to explain what I had learned. How the Lord taught me to really pray and how he had healed me. I watched everything on TV that had anything to do with healing or being filled with the Spirit. I know it was hard for David to understand. I was morphing into this "I can't get enough of the Word, praying all the time, quoting scriptures all the time" woman. I was on fire with passion for the truth! He had seen me sick in bed so long, now I was like a rocket, ready to launch at any moment. How could he understand? No one we knew was like me. It was probably a little scary for him, now that I think about it.

I prayed for him a lot. He didn't want to talk about my healing much. I was healed; he was grateful. Now let's move on with life. As a matter of fact, no one really wanted to talk about my healing much. I was so joyful and excited but there were not many friends to be joyful with.

Thank the Lord for my friend Marty! She would talk about it with me. She may not have understood it all—I didn't either!—but she believed it and listened to me.

Marty told me not long ago, "I still remember you hobbling up and down those stairs. I felt so sorry for you." I don't remember many details, it's been so long. I just remember the pain and agony in my mind.

It was hard in the months after the healing to go to church. No one mentioned healing to me much. If I mentioned it, they were "so glad" and dropped the subject. I couldn't blame them; they didn't know how to respond. They had no teaching on the subject; there was no frame of reference. That makes people fearful. They consider it off the deep end. Well, if it was, then I was "off" and it was lonely.

I was healed completely in August and the church had a women's retreat in fall. Marty and I decided we'd go. The weather was gorgeous. Red and gold leaves dancing in cool sunshine. It was my favorite time of the year, and I was ready to enjoy it!

The camp was out in the country, with rustic but comfortable rooms. There was a sweet stone chapel and a bookstore. Crisp leaves crackled under our feet as we walked the colorful grounds.

Our Friday night speaker was a lady who spoke at women's conferences nationwide. I was kind of excited. I was even more excited, I think, about getting away, outdoors, and being refreshed.

Marty and I went to the meeting after dinner. Enthusiastic women packed out the chapel. Our speaker took the platform, and after a few formal words to the host churches, she started telling us about the trials in her life. She had recently had gone through a very difficult trial. She had a baby about a year old when she got very sick.

As she started describing symptoms, the pain, the testing, the diagnosis, Marty and I couldn't believe it! I grabbed Marty's hand. It was Sarcoidosis! The same disease God had just healed me of. The speaker said she was learning to live with this trial and disease and God was using it in her life.

I felt flushed. My nerves started fluttering in my stomach.

As we know, the Bible says He uses all things in our lives, good and bad, when we belong to Him (Romans 8:28 Paige paraphrase). I understood that. But I knew that sickness did not come from God. I had just lived through the same nightmare. My excitement began to build. I couldn't wait to get out of that chapel and talk to her!

I felt like I was on fire. I could help this woman! Maybe God had sent me here just for this. My mind was rushing, rehearsing words.

Marty was right with me. I said, "I've got to go talk to her!"

"Please, go on!" she said. We spotted the speaker in the crowd afterward as people milled at the refreshments tables. She was standing next to my pastor's wife, a lovely, godly woman.

I walked up to them, even though at the same time I wanted to run; I couldn't wait. "Excuse me," I said. "I was listening to your story. I had that same disease and the Lord healed me."

My pastor's wife went a little gray. She physically turned the speaker around and said, "Excuse us. We have to go over here and do something."

She looked back at me like I was imbalanced or nuts. I couldn't believe it! I felt like she dumped a bucket of ice water over my head.

I walked numbly back to our room. All the loveliness of the night and the crisp air didn't matter anymore. I went to bed confused and crying out to God. The next morning questions whirled through my mind, and I told Marty I couldn't go to hear the speaker.

I cried out to God again, "Lord, why did You heal me? Why doesn't anyone want to hear about how You heal? Healing is so awesome! What's wrong with people?" I felt so down my spirit. I knew the fire was still there, but it is amazing how others' words and attitudes can squelch a fire if you let it.

At lunch I decided to venture out for a walk. I passed the bookstore where our speaker was browsing the books, alone. I didn't even think. I slowly went in and sidled up next to her.

"Hi. My name is Paige Jackson," I said. She was very glad to meet me and was a very personable lady. I said, "You know last night, I just wanted to tell you how the Lord healed me of the same disease you said you had." In my mind I think if I had heard those words I would have replied with "Really, that's awesome, tell me all about it. I'm so excited."

She smiled and kept looking through the books. "Well, I believe this is how the Lord keeps me humble." She said a few other things too, but I don't remember them.

I could hardly speak. I said goodbye, somehow, and returned to my room. I felt sick to my stomach. This was not a retreat, it was torment. In the blur of it now, I can't remember even going to any more sessions.

Marty and I discussed it on the way home. We both felt kind of blurry in our thinking. If someone is sick, why wouldn't they want to get well? If I had said, "I know of a new drug that treats Sarcoidosis very well" the information would have been accepted.

The Bible says, "Humble yourselves in the sight of the Lord and He will lift you up" (James 4:10). The idea that a devastating sickness could bring humility was a new idea to me. It seemed to me that devastating sickness was destruction in every area of life. It stole from your body, your time, your money, your family, and on and on.

Maybe it would make people feel more humble. Maybe

people would have more compassion for the sick, but what is God highest purpose for us?

The Bible doesn't say He wants to keep us sick, poor and needy so we will be humble. Jesus said, "When you see me, you see the Father" (John 14:9 Paige paraphrase). Jesus did what the Father did. If you were to black out all the scriptures in the New Testament where Jesus talked about healing or healed people or the disciples healed people, there would be whole sections missing! Jesus came to save and heal and make people whole.

He wants us to be humble and come to Him with our needs and desires, not be haughty and think we can save ourselves or live life on our own.

Humble Yourself

I've heard of people's lives turning around when someone in their family gets sick, but the Bible says, "The goodness of God leads us to repentance" (Romans 2:4). We are drawn by His love, not fever or tornados or losing everything we own.

Now in the earth and in the Bible are plenty of stories about people who ignore God, then some awful tragedy comes about in their lives and they finally give in, humble themselves and decide to follow God. True.

I'm just speculating, but if I were standing before the God who made heaven and earth, and I asked Him, "Lord do You want me to come to You freely to repent when I sin or would You rather some destruction hit me and those I love so You can show us something first and then I come to You?" What do you think He would say?

Either way, I know He would say He wants us. That's not a question. He wants us full of faith. He wants us when we are weary and needy. He just wants us! He instructs us to come as we are (Isaiah 1:18; Revelation 22:17). If we really look at the message of the Word we see His best plan for us. We receive everything He has done for us: forgiveness, healing, blessing, abundance.

I decided after that retreat I did not have all the answers. I *did* know from the Word that God wants people well. You can discuss the subject "ten ways to Sunday," but God's son Jesus gave His life so we could be saved from our sins. He was beaten for our healing. I believed it; it was right there in black and white in my Bible (Isaiah 53).

I thought I was alone in my belief, but I wasn't.

What I Believe

I now believe that sickness has no right in a Christian's body. It is a trespasser. Some people think, *Oh these people who believe in healing just say they are not sick.* I say, if you have symptoms of green snot running down your face, or fever or a bad report from the doctor, sickness has no right in your body!

We as Christians are purchased by the blood of Jesus. The Word says He bore our sickness on the cross for us (Matthew 8:17). He came into the world and healed all manner of disease. He hated disease while He was on the earth and He still hates it. He is the same yesterday, today, and forever (Hebrews 13:8). He did not say when He left the disciples, "I'm going away now to be with my Father. Sorry guys, the healing bit is over." No! He said, "Heal the sick, raise the dead, and cast out demons" (Matthew 10:8).

He is the same loving Jesus with the same loving Father. It is the same Holy Spirit who lives in us that lived in the disciples on the day of Pentecost. Even when the disciples' shadows touched people they were healed. Wow! That is what we should all want as Christians. We should not say healing is gone. Healing is for today and always.

34

Psalm 16:11 KJV

Thou wilt shew me the path of life: in thy presence is fullness of joy; at thy right hand there are pleasures for evermore.

5

THE PRESENCE OF GOD

David gradually began to accept my seemingly erratic behavior. Filled with excitement about God's promises, I had a hard time keeping my mouth shut. I tried not to tell *every*one, but everywhere I turned, someone was sick. Someone needed to know the truth about God's heart and what He had already done for us. So I talked to a few friends, prayed and waited.

I remind myself of Thomas Edison. He invented the light bulb, working on it for years and years, day and night. People didn't have much interest. They thought he was a little eccentric or cracked in the head...until he turned the light on. I suppose it is a little tongue-in-cheek, but "then they saw the light."

I'm not comparing myself to Edison; I'm just saying that until people see miracles and healings, the light of understanding doesn't come on, unless God Himself opens their eyes to see the light.

While in this season of waiting, our pastor began a series of sermons about spiritual gifts mentioned in the Word. He was a knowledgeable man, but when he came to the supernatural gifts like healing and miracles, he just left them out, like they weren't even there.

That really frustrated David. He had come to the point where he wasn't sure about it all, but decided if it was in the Word then it needed to be addressed. He wanted to learn and know!

The Invitation

David had been invited three times that same week to a small Church of God not far from our house. We had probably passed it a hundred times and never noticed it. Feeling a little anxious, we decided to visit on a Wednesday night. It was very small, seating about 150 people.

That Wednesday night there were about three or four visitors and maybe 10 other people plus the song leader and the pastor whom we had never met. Not too impressive.

When the singing started we could feel a heaviness in the atmosphere. We both cried at different times during worship. There were tissue boxes at the end of each pew.

The pastor preached like I'd never heard before. He preached his heart out; the Word was alive. I can identify it now as the anointing; the Holy Spirit was there in power. The glory of God was present, and we were there with the other 13 people. I looked around and thought, *I've never heard the Word preached like that! Where are all the people?*

We joined this small congregation every Wednesday night for a month. We cried every week. I only talk about that because I had never felt the presence of God. I had heard about His presence, even sang about it, but I didn't know anyone who actually felt it!

His Presence

One night I invited one of my closest friends who had really been seeking God to come with me. I said, "Now if you cry, it's all right. It is just the Holy Spirit." She didn't understand, of course. Not yet.

As soon as we sat down, the music started. She wept and wept. I just smiled at her through my own tears.

I had spent so many years of my life in church. I had studied the Word, taught children's church and Sunday school and heard hundreds of sermons, but had never felt the loving presence of God. In God's presence every weight falls away and you feel His love overwhelming you. We were being washed and refreshed.

Then we started going to this little church on Sundays too. Sunday mornings and evenings. Even special services. We couldn't get enough. It was wonderful!

The church drew the poor and wealthy, homosexuals and drug addicts. People were getting saved every week. They were being set free from sickness, oppression and addiction. It was heaven! David and I were both excited. It was a great place to be. We had never heard such truth.

We heard about people who preached the "full gospel" like Oral Roberts and Reinhard Bonnke. We heard about movements of the Holy Spirit like Azuza Street and the Welch Revival. But experiencing it was all new to us. We were around like-minded people who were seeking God just like us.

One week it was announced that on Thursday nights a series on "Power Evangelism" would be taught. It was a video series about John Wimber, the founder of the Vineyard Movement. In this movement thousands of people had been healed. They taught people how to pray for the sick.

I just had to go! I felt like a dog salivating over food. David stayed home with the boys and encouraged me to go.

Every Thursday I would leave the meeting and cry all the way home. I cried, "Oh God, I just want to pray for the sick! Let me do it, Lord! I want to see healings, signs and wonders!" I tried to raise my hand while I was driving, which wasn't a great idea. My heart burned with desire to be used and flooded with compassion to see people healed from all diseases.

God just had to use me. He had let me live, surely He would use me.

The final Thursday night I prayed but had no idea what was ahead. The very next day, Friday, my life changed drastically again.

I Peter 5:8

Be sober, be vigilant; because your
adversary the devil walks about like a
roaring lion, seeking whom he may devour.

6

"SATAN, YOU LEAVE ME ALONE IN JESUS' NAME"

It was Friday morning. The kids went to school, David went to work, and I was praying. All was usual.

Our kitchen floor was linoleum and had tiny holes in it from age and wear. It was time to go by the carpet store and look at their selection of flooring.

A salesman came up to help me. He was nice, and I still remember his name 27 years later. He did not stand out in his appearance, just a normal person in his mid-thirties. I decided on a pattern that wouldn't show a lot of dirt. He was accommodating and would come out on Friday of that week to measure the floor.

> —I pray for you right now, that you will see, hear and grasp and put into practice the truths that come from this situation and that you will be set free and live free!—

I left the carpet store in my car and immediately starting experiencing the most bizarre thoughts. Random thoughts like *what if I ever did anything with that salesman?*

I must have a pretty Puritanical mind, because just having the thought scared me. I wondered *Why would I think something like that? I love David. That man wasn't even attractive. Why would I ever think that?*

What is funny looking back, but wasn't funny then, is that I never thought about *what* I'd do with someone else, I thought "*What if?*" And those two words were enough to send me into a tailspin of fear and torment that I had never experienced before.

I was a Christian. I loved the Lord. I served the Lord—as far as I knew—with my whole heart. I'd been healed. I loved my husband. I was shocked by this incident and it consumed me for days. I could never tell David; what would he think of me?

Even Ice Cream and Stop Signs Came From a Thought

This thought had been cast into my mind and I thought about "what if" for a week. *What if I ever did anything with this man?* It may sound weak, but it was real to me.

Thoughts are powerful. Everything that we see started with a thought. The earth itself started with God's thoughts and declarations. Inventions start with a thought or idea. Everything from vanilla ice cream to a stop sign came from a thought. The Bible says as a man thinks in his heart, so is he. (Proverbs 23:7 Paige paraphrase). I felt lower than scum. I was a mother and wife; I was an on fire Christian. What was wrong with me?

I told David I would really like for him to be at home when this salesman came to measure. He said, "Oh, it's okay. You can handle it." He was too busy. I was really fearful. I asked David several times. Then I talked to myself. I told myself how silly I was being, and to snap out of it, to put my fears aside.

Friday morning the doorbell rang. I was fine.

The man was a demure person, and he never really looked me in the eye. He talked but kept his head down, intent on the flooring job. As he was leaving, he noticed we had a hot tub on the deck. Without looking at me he said, "You know, one time I was in a lady's house who had a hot tub and she stripped down naked and jumped in it right in front of me."

Well, I wasn't afraid, but I sure didn't know how to respond! I muttered something jokingly. He got to the front door, then the front porch. As he was stepping onto the sidewalk, he turned around and started telling me—out of the blue—that he is having marital problems. I was backing up to shut the door. Then he tells me he is a youth director at a small church.

I said, "Thank you so much, so sorry," and shut the door as quickly as possible.

Flabbergasted and shocked, I just stood there with my back against the door! I didn't know what was going on.

Now I know there was a battle going on. It was for my mind and ultimately for my life. I had no idea what I was about to walk through. I wasn't feeling the presence of God now. I was feeling confusion and fear.

I still didn't tell David. That is not something you tell your husband, even once in a lifetime! What would I tell him anyway? I wasn't attracted to the man. But still, I was plagued with "what if" I was tormented with this thought, though I had still not even thought about what "what if" was.

I was barraged constantly. Like the record of my thoughts was stuck on a skip in my head. Something had opened the door for the Accuser.

Revelation 12:10b describes how Satan is the "accuser of our brethren (who) accused them before our God day and night." This was exactly what I was experiencing, day and night, constant accusation of *what if.*

I hadn't done anything. Didn't want to, wasn't going to, so why did I keep thinking these two little words, *what if?* If the *what if* had had any substance I would have really felt bad.

Darkness into Light

Finally I remembered a scriptural principle, when you bring darkness into light, the enemy can't hold it against you (based on I Corinthians 4:5). I knew I had to tell David. I had to get this off my heart and mind.

One night I finally blurted out the whole story that had been going on for a couple of weeks by then. His response was awesome!

"Well," he said, "when you were big and pregnant with Corey, I was kind of attracted to this lady who worked in our office and wore a black and white polka dot dress one day. It didn't mean anything. It was no big deal."

Those were his words that dispelled my fears. "It was no big deal." He had been attracted to a non-pregnant woman and I was just dealing with *what if* with someone I wasn't at all attracted to. I was excited. I was relieved! "Really?" I acted like it was a good thing. Like David said, it was No Big Deal.

The torment was gone. The burden was gone. Bringing my dark thoughts into the light was freedom!

The next week I was doing something with Brice and had the thought, *what if I ever hurt one of my children?* It was like a flash in my mind, *Where did that thought come from?*

I was devastated again. *Why would I think that? What kind of a person am I?* It kicked of a cycle of torturous thinking again. I was one of the most devoted mothers I knew. I had asked the Lord to let me live and raise my boys.

He did. Why would I think that? There it was again, *what if?*

I let that *what if* rumble around in my head for weeks, so ashamed. I could never tell anyone that! *Am I an awful person?* I cried out to God and prayed constantly. I was tormented again.

I couldn't take it. This self-condemnation was terrible. I remembered what I'd done before in telling David. I had lost weight, couldn't sleep. I thought, *People who love Jesus don't think this way!* So I said, "I have to tell you something."

Again, when I brought darkness into the light it caused the thought to have no power over me. David talked to me about how silly it was. He prayed for me and I was free. The torment was gone again!

I went through a few weeks of freedom, but the enemy was still on the rampage. One night I saw a commercial on TV and had the thought *What if I'm a lesbian?* You may be thinking "how ridiculous." It was ridiculous! In light of the situation in the world today, many people may even think, "so what?" In my world it was not acceptable to me. The Bible clearly stated to me that women should love men and men should love women. Adam was given Eve in the Garden, he was not given another Adam or "Steve." That is just the way it is when you believe the Bible, and I do. The downward spiral began again.

That time it was really bad. That was something I could never tell David. I lost down to 116 pounds and hardly slept at all.

Fear Instead of Faith

You see, fear had taken the place of the faith I was walking in. Faith was relegated to the backseat and fear was driving my life.

My mind spun with thoughts like *They are going to put you away*—whoever "they" are. *I won't be able to raise my children.* The same record kept playing over and over in my head.

Of course, David knew something was wrong. He was probably noticing my big mood shifts. Finally one day we were walking in the neighborhood. I said the words I'm sure he didn't want to hear, "I have to tell you something."

He said, "OK."

"I had this thought the other day," I said, "what if I'm a lesbian, and it's been bothering me all the time." (*What if* again!)

David laughed out loud. He didn't even stop to think how it would affect me. He said, "Is there anything you haven't thought?"

Tears blurred my vision as I said, "I don't think so."

That's when he said again, "That's ridiculous!" We prayed and talked as we walked. I felt the overwhelming heaviness lift again. Light had penetrated the darkness and I was free!

During all these months of mental oppression (I know what to call it now), I had been in lots of prayer lines. I couldn't stand to go to church. I cried all the time in church. People would ask me what was wrong and I was too ashamed to tell. I'd say, "Just pray for me." I can't ever remember leaving the church free. I left just as burdened as when I'd walked in.

I gave up teaching children's church which I'd been teaching a long time. I told the leaders I was sorry. I was trying to cope with life. I was barely coping with my own kids. Corey was 10 and Brice was 6. They never knew I was suffering.

After all the tormenting thoughts were gone, I was left with what I call "the icky feeling." It would come over me sometimes and I couldn't sleep, so I called this sweet lady from our church, sometimes at 2:00 in the morning. She was gracious. She would pray for me and tell it to leave. Then I'd go back to sleep, but it would come back.

I had thought I was depressed or something was imbalanced. I went to a Bible study where the ladies would pray for me to sleep and I would, but there was no peace and certainly no joy. It had been about a year and a half. I was better, but it wasn't over.

A friend of mine invited me to a women's Aglow meeting. Aglow was known for great speakers from around the world. This special speaker was from Arkansas and was supposed to be amazing. I was ready for amazing! So I went.

Fighting the Devil Every Day

When the altar call came, I went up—Again!! I can't tell you how many prayer lines I'd been in by this time. I thought about not going up, but there I went, me, the woman who talked to everyone about healing. Me, the one who talked about faith all the time to everyone I met. I was at the bottom of a pit.

I saw the speaker at a distance. The line was quite long. She was probably in her 50's and showed a lot of compassion for people as she prayed for their needs.

I finally reached her. She took my hands and I told her about the tormenting thoughts, the harassment, the sleeplessness.

I'll never forget what she said. "Honey, you got to learn to fight the devil every day." She told me part of her story, which I don't remember, and prayed for me.

On the way home in the car, I had a revelation of truth. I had suffered for a year and a half. I said, "Lord, that's it! It's not me, I'm not crazy! It's the devil! He's trying to kill me!"

Hosea 4:6a My people are destroyed for lack of knowledge.

This scripture doesn't just mean people go to hell when they don't know about Jesus dying on the cross for their sins. It means also that there are certain principles in the Bible that can extend our lives and cause us to be blessed.

For example according to Ephesians 6:2 if children honor their parents it (life) will go well with them. And Genesis 12:3 says if we bless Israel, we will be blessed. There are many more examples.

Before that day, I knew about the devil, but not a lot. No one ever talked much about his tactics. I never had much teaching about him except that he would be thrown into the lake of fire at the end of time.

I started focusing my mind on who I am in Christ according to the Word. I am an heir to the throne of God (Romans 8:17). I am a child of God (John 1:12). All His plans for me are good (Jeremiah 29:11). I lack no good thing (Psalm 34:10).

Satan is a defeated foe. The Lord says in Isaiah 54:17, "'No weapon formed against you shall prosper, And every tongue *which* rises against you in judgment You shall condemn. This *is* the heritage of the servants of the Lord, And their righteousness *is* from Me,' Says the Lord."

I had allowed Satan to steal from me, like the enemy he is, as if he were a robber standing in my house with a weapon. In my ignorance I had allowed him in to torment and harass me. But no longer!

You see, I had received lots of prayer with temporary results. Many Christians I knew that loved me and some I didn't know had prayed for me diligently. I had opened the door to demonic attacks by believing the words *what if*.

Those words have no power.

It's much like if someone throws you a baseball. You can

catch it or let it fall to the ground. I had caught those words and been ensnared by those words. Now I knew, and I was willing to fight!

Willing to Fight

I went home and in my kitchen every morning I would point at an unseen enemy and say, "Satan, you leave me alone in the name of Jesus. I will not think those thoughts!" I couldn't see him or his demons, but they were there, waiting for me to give in.

I was learning to stand, again. Sometimes the thoughts would come in like a flood. Every day, all through the day, I would do the same thing. I'd speak the same sentence out loud to a foe I could not see.

The devil cannot read our thoughts. He can only hear what we say and use it against us. I had said plenty he could use.

Resist the Devil and He Has to Flee

Every day I stood with a new resolve. A boldness overtook me. I knew I was victorious in the name of Jesus. I thought to myself and then said out loud, "If I have to do this the rest of my life, I will. Satan, you leave me alone in the name of Jesus!" I really had no deadline in mind.

As with my healing experience, I had not walked this way before, and I didn't really know the perfect way to do things or say things. I just knew according to the Word that if I resisted the devil he would flee from me, so I was going to resist.

James 4:7b Resist the devil and he will flee from you.

I didn't think, *Oh, I'll do this a few times and he will leave me alone.* This was war! And if I had to do it forever, well, then I would be fighting for my life. I knew later it wasn't just for me. It was for the life of many others too.

You see, Satan was defeated when Jesus died on the cross. The Bible says in

Ephesians 6:12 For we do not wrestle against flesh and blood, but against principalities, against powers, against the rulers of the darkness of this age, against spiritual *hosts* of wickedness in the heavenly *places.*

I began to learn to put on the armor of God from Ephesians 6. You can make the declaration easy to remember by putting it on in order from top to bottom: "I put on the helmet of salvation, the breastplate of righteousness, the belt of truth. I shod my feet with the preparation of the gospel of peace. I take the shield of faith and the sword of the spirit (which is the Word of God) and go forth in Jesus' name."

I knew all this in my head, but I was getting the revelation down into my spirit, again. It was just the truth. The devil is defeated. He is under Jesus' feet, and so he is under our feet, because we are in Christ. We have to recognize the enemy when he comes in like a roaring lion (I Peter 5:8).

I recognized later that the man in the carpet store had a spirit of lust. That spirit bothered me so much that it opened me up to a spirit of fear.

II Timothy 1:7 For God has not given us a spirit of fear, but of power and of love and of a sound mind.

Since God has not given us a spirit of fear, when fear rushes in, my mind seemed unsound. I had believed a lie from the enemy. It was a pretty tricky lie. It sounded like me. It was kind of like Satan's question to Eve in the Garden, "Did God really say...?" (Genesis 3:1).

The enemy didn't have to tell a blatant lie, just twist things. If I had known this in the beginning I could have stood my ground then, told fear to leave and walked on with life without the torment.

This experience had gone on too long. I had not prayed for anyone to be healed in a year and a half. I had hardly prayed for anyone else. I had been totally consumed with me. I had not known I had authority in Jesus' name and at my voice, the enemy had to flee.

For two weeks I spoke out against the unseen enemy all day long. Suddenly one day I realized I was free. There was no fear. No fear of *what if*, or anything else.

I had not given up. I was free!

It surprised me. I had been fighting a long time. Now my mind was clear, there was no condemnation left. I knew it was over.

The enemy sought to devour me, (I Peter 5:8) but God was faithful (Psalm 89:8 among a myriad), my very present help in time of trouble (Psalm 46:1). The Word says to cast "down imaginations, and every high thing that exalteth itself against the knowledge of God, and bringing into captivity every thought to the obedience of Christ (II Corinthians 10:5 KJV). Now I know and have practiced this truth for years.

It might be fear about my body or my children or relationships, but I say, "Lord, I cast that fear down in Jesus' name. It will not linger here. I give this situation to You." I may have to tell Satan to leave me alone—but I don't have to fight like I did before.

This part of my life was hard, but the Lord uses all things in our lives for our good and His glory. He used this lesson of learning to fight in Jesus' name many times in my life and the lives of others. Many people I've talked to are set free now, because they know they have authority in Jesus' name.

I Samuel 12:37

Moreover David said, "The LORD, who delivered me from the paw of the lion and from the paw of the bear, He will deliver me from the hand of this Philistine."

7

WARRIOR CHILD

Most times when we go through trials in our lives we are crying out to God for relief. We cry out for Him to get us out of the problem, to stop the pain. I remember going through several trials, and I'd say, "Lord, I don't want to go through this…I don't want to help anybody in the future." I actually said these words. That was pretty selfish, but physical pain or oppression hurt. During these times, feeling tortured, I didn't care if I ever helped anyone.

God must really chuckle to Himself when we toss up these careless statements, because He knows us better than we know ourselves.

My whole life I've wanted to help and rescue people, but when I was actually walking through the "valley of the shadow," my heart and mind were screaming, "Get me out of here!"

Why would I think that way? I really knew I would help people. All the things I was learning in these dark places God would use later to pull others out of their dark pits of despair.

After I was free in my body and mind, I had a testimony that other people needed to hear. I was really ready—after a while—to shout it to the nations. But, even in their dark hour, some people are not ready to hear. They are stuck in a religious mindset or they just don't believe change is available. In reality, they don't *want* to stay where they are, but they are afraid to step out and apply the Word. Some people think it is all emotion. Some people have asked me if I had faith in my faith when I was healed. I would reply, "No. It's all about Jesus and the Word." I used the faith He gave me and it increased as I learned the Word. Having faith in faith won't save you. Won't heal your body. Won't release you from demonic oppression.

A few people knew about the oppression I was going through, but not many. It's not something you want to broadcast. It's not something you can explain in words. My children did not even know.

My opportunity to help someone came up quickly.

I had a new outlook. I had a new perspective. I knew and felt with all my heart that God was for me and not against me (Romans 8:31). I knew He was almighty (Exodus 6:3). I knew He freely gives us all things that pertain to life and godliness (II Peter 1:3). I knew I had authority on the earth because of the blood of Jesus (Revelation 12:11) and the name of Jesus (John 20:31).

I was in a great place. Freedom in my mind and body tasted good! I was "singing a new song" in my heart. Then the enemy hit my youngest son with disturbing thoughts. I was facing the same battle, the ugly giant of fear all over again.

I had no idea that the experience I had just been through would be used by God to deliver my son, and others.

My youngest, Brice, was very sensitive when he was little. He was one of those sweet little boys who played by himself. He never argued. He had a deep sense of spiritual things at a young age.

He wanted to ask Jesus to be his Savior at four years old.

We were sitting at the kitchen table, his face solemn. He started telling me that he had sinned. I said, "What have you done?" He couldn't think of anything, but he knew he had.

We were not a family that talked about sin much. Our Sunday school probably mentioned it now and then, but not a lot.

He was very persistent that day, so we talked about what it meant to be a Christian and what the Bible says we are to do. He desperately wanted to ask Jesus into his heart.

As we talked I couldn't imagine telling a child "No, you can't become a Christian, you don't know enough about it yet." The Bible says come as a little child (Matthew 18:4 Paige paraphrase). So Brice prayed and asked Jesus to be his Savior. I know he was saved then, and he was so excited to have Jesus in his heart.

I prayed later, "Lord, if I've missed it anywhere or we didn't do everything right will You come, in whatever way You want to, and set things straight with him?" I had to trust God.

When Brice was seven years old we were at church one Sunday morning and a friend of his asked if Brice could go home with him for the afternoon to play. We knew the mom very well. The little friend was sweet and obedient so we said yes.

At church that night, Brice sat between David and me, whispering during the service.

"Mom, I want to talk to you."

"Not yet. We'll talk after church."

He kept on and on, saying, "But, I have to!"

"It can wait until after church" I kept saying

Finally he said desperately, "I have to. It's about sex."

David and I shot each other alarming looks over his head. Our 11-year-old son, Corey, rolled his eyes and scooted a little further away from us, already wise to the subject.

With Corey, David and I got to choose a time to approach

the subject of the birds and the bees. We prayed. We had a wonderful book to go through with him by a Christian author. All went smoothly.

After church in the car we sat listening. Brice kept saying, "I've got to talk." He was very upset. We went by McDonalds' because we had promised them a snack. Corey had had about all he could stand and told Brice to shut up.

"As soon as we get home we will talk," I said.

We got home and Corey escaped to his room as fast as he could. The three of us sat quietly in the den.

Brice began by saying he and his friend found a book in his friend's teenage brother's room, under the bed. It had pictures in it. Well, you can imagine where the conversation went. He had never heard anything about where babies come from. Now his innocent mind was bombarded with images from this book.

I took out the book I had used to talk to Corey. It was all about how God made creatures, animals, and humans, to multiply on the earth He had created. I would turn the page and say, "See here are the bees and flowers; here's mommy horses and baby horses." He would say, "That's not it." I could tell David would have liked to slip out of the room, but he knew I needed him there.

"Here's a momma dog and a puppy." He shook his head, "That's not it."

I felt flushed. He wanted me to hurry through the cats, pigs, goats and chickens. Finally there was a human mom and dad. They got married and God gave them a baby.

That was fine, but he wanted the details. So we had to tell him. There's no telling what he saw in that book under the bed, and we wanted him to hear about it from God's perspective. He was so young. I felt it was unfair for him to be shoved into this knowledge when he wasn't emotionally ready. We would just have to deal with it. We all prayed together and went to bed.

The next few weeks and months were hard for him, and us. He would come into the kitchen, such a sweet little face greeting us, and he'd sadly say, "I'm thinking about that stuff again." We would pray together and I would talk to him about it being a beautiful plan that God had for people. It wasn't beautiful to him. I was glad that he felt free to talk to us. I did not want him ever to feel shame over this.

He would see a commercial on TV with girls and say, "Mom, I'm thinking about that stuff again." He was vexed and tormented most of the time.

We could have taken him to counseling, but it would have been more embarrassing for him. We prayed every time the thoughts would hit him.

After about a month of praying and finding no relief, I decided to tell him a bit of my experience with tormenting thoughts and how God showed me what to do. Since I was totally free from the tormenting thoughts, I could tell him at that point.

Even at a young age he understood because of what he was going through. This was not a game to him. He was serious about wanting to be free.

I didn't give a lot of details, I just said "I was having disturbing thoughts in the past, and God showed me it wasn't me. The devil is a thought caster. He shoots thoughts into people's minds and they think they are a bad person. They think the thoughts are theirs."

The Bible says in II Corinthians 10:5 in the Paige paraphrase, "cast down every imagination that exalts itself above the name of Christ." Imaginations that are tormenting have to bow at the name of Jesus. We have authority over them in Jesus' name!

Brice knew Jesus was living in him and he knew how powerful Jesus is, so he believed it without question.

I told him "It is fighting an enemy, like in cartoons, but this enemy you can't see."

So the journey began. I would hear him upstairs in his room playing, then he would stop and say in a loud voice. "Satan, you leave me alone in the name of Jesus. I will not think those thoughts." A few hours later I would hear him again, "Satan, you leave me alone in the name of Jesus. I will not think those thoughts."

My Warrior Child

I remember standing in the foyer one day. I could hear him upstairs. He was seven and he was a warrior already. I was crying. It made me sad he was going through this, but I knew he would get through.

Now you might think this was concentrating too much on Satan, but it wasn't. Brice would be riding in the car and the thoughts would pop into his head. "Satan, you leave me alone in the name of Jesus. I will not think those thoughts," he would say. It was grieving to him. He hated it, so he learned to do battle.

We talked about putting on the full armor of God (Ephesians 6). He understood that and we would put it on together. We played audio scriptures in his room because he knew the Word of God had power.

If (future King) David could kill a giant at age 14 or 15, and Samuel could go into temple service before the Lord at age 3, then Brice would learn to be a mighty little warrior at age 7.

The enemy was relentless, so we were relentless.

Brice told me one day when he was a few years older, "You know mom, remember when I battled the enemy, it lasted eight months." I had forgotten. He hadn't.

It was a spiritual lesson in life he had to learn so young. He wasn't alone. We were there with him and God was guiding us.

We don't all walk the same path. These lessons we learn are for us, and for people who need help along our way.

> **Revelation 12:11** And they overcame him by the blood of the Lamb and by the word of their testimony...

Overcomers

When we overcome, Jesus says of us:

> **Revelation 3:5** I will not blot out his name from the Book of Life; but I will confess his name before My Father and before His angels.

> **Revelation 3:12 & 21** He who overcomes, I will make him a pillar in the temple of My God, and he shall go out no more. I will write on him the name of My God and the name of the city of My God, the New Jerusalem, which comes down out of heaven from My God. And *I will write on him* My new name... To him who overcomes I will grant to sit with Me on My throne, as I also overcame and sat down with My Father on His throne.

Since we overcome like Jesus overcame, we will get to sit with Jesus, just at Jesus sits with His Father on His throne!

We might think overcoming just means salvation, but here on earth we walk it out, not to gain salvation—salvation is freely given—but to walk in freedom here. The devil may be stalking us as a roaring lion, but he is already defeated. We are victorious. Jesus overcame so we overcome. We must walk out the victory. The devil wants us to give up and give in because life is hard. The devil wants us to live in fear and depression, to be sick in our bodies, and to lack peace. That's when we take the Word as our weapon and prove we are an overcomer in this life.

> **Romans 8:31b** If God *is* for us, who *can be* against us?

> **Acts 17:28a** for in Him we live and move and have our being.

> **I Corinthians 2:16b** but we have the mind of Christ.

Resist the Devil

So since God said, "Resist the devil, and he will flee from you" (James 4:7), we resisted the devil. Now you may resist the enemy by not looking at evil magazines or not being around the wrong kind of influences, or putting down the dozen doughnuts if you need to lose 30 pounds. Sometimes we have to resist him out loud. The enemy can't read our minds. He only knows what he hears us saying. We don't carry on a conversation with him; we just resist him.

That's what I did, not fully understanding. That's what Brice did, not fully understanding. We could only do it because God helped us. God hears every little cry, every little prayer. It is He who gives us strength and grace to stand.

I think about a cartoon of the little dog with a bone I once saw. A big ugly dog comes up and tries to steal the little dog's bone. The little dog growls ferociously and finally the big dog, his tail between his legs, yelps and runs away. The little dog looks proud, wagging his little tail. He lies down in peace, gnawing on his bone. He is satisfied that he scared away the big dog. But what the little dog doesn't see, is that his daddy was behind him—the whole time.

That is kind of the way I think about God. We are standing, praying, fighting. He hears us and sends his mighty angels to back us up, strengthening us, keeping us safe. I like to think He wraps us up in His robe.

We were singing a worship song a few Sundays ago about Jesus wrapping us up in his arms and I saw a picture in my mind as I worshipped of me holding onto Jesus. He wrapped His big white cloak around me. All I could see was my head on His shoulder. He was hugging me close. I peeked out from the covering that almost covered my face. There were bears, lions and darkness all around. But I felt safe. I turned my head a little and stuck my tongue out at them, like a little child would in her daddy's arms. It was as if to say, "I don't care what you do, how loud you growl or snarl to try to intimidate me, this is my Dad and I am safe in His arms.

Who can defeat the Lord our God?

Psalm 118:5-6 I called on the LORD in distress;
The LORD answered me *and set me* in a broad place.
[6] The LORD *is* on my side; I will not fear.
What can man do to me?

Verses to Stand on Deliverance and Protection

Psalm 9:9-10 The LORD also will be a refuge for the oppressed, A refuge in times of trouble. [10] And those who know Your name will put their trust in You; For You, LORD, have not forsaken those who seek You.

Psalm 17:7 Show Your marvelous lovingkindness by Your right hand,
O You who save those who trust *in You*
From those who rise up *against them.*

Psalm 18:30 *As for* God, His way *is* perfect; The word of the LORD is proven; He *is* a shield to all who trust in Him.

Psalm 18:48 He delivers me from my enemies.
You also lift me up above those who rise against me;
You have delivered me from the violent man.

Psalm 27:13 *I would have lost heart,* unless I had believed That I would see the goodness of the LORD In the land of the living.

Psalm 28:7 The LORD *is* my strength and my shield; My heart trusted in Him, and I am helped; Therefore my heart greatly rejoices, And with my song I will praise Him

Psalm 32:7 You *are* my hiding place; You shall preserve me from trouble;
You shall surround me with songs of deliverance…Selah

Psalm 34:17 *The righteous* cry out, and the LORD hears,
And delivers them out of all their troubles

Psalm 37:40 And the LORD shall help them and deliver them;
He shall deliver them from the wicked, And save them,
Because they trust in Him.

Psalm 41:11 By this I know that You are well pleased with
me, Because my enemy does not triumph over me.

Psalm 57:1 Be merciful to me, O God, be merciful to me!
For my soul trusts in You; And in the shadow of Your wings I
will make my refuge,
Until *these* calamities have passed by.

Psalm 59:9 I will wait for You, O You his Strength; For God
is my defense.

Psalm 68: 1-4 Let God arise, Let His enemies be scattered;
Let those also who hate Him flee before Him. [2] As smoke is
driven away, So drive *them* away; As wax melts before the
fire, *So* let the wicked perish at the presence of God.
[3] But let the righteous be glad; Let them rejoice before God;
Yes, let them rejoice exceedingly.
[4] Sing to God, sing praises to His name; Extol Him who rides
on the clouds, By His name YAH, And rejoice before Him.

Psalm 91
He who dwells in the secret place of the Most High
Shall abide under the shadow of the Almighty.
[2] I will say of the LORD, *"He is* my refuge and my fortress;
My God, in Him I will trust."

[3] Surely He shall deliver you from the snare of the fowler
And from the perilous pestilence.

⁴ He shall cover you with His feathers,
And under His wings you shall take refuge;
His truth *shall be your* shield and buckler.
⁵ You shall not be afraid of the terror by night,
Nor of the arrow *that* flies by day,
⁶ *Nor* of the pestilence *that* walks in darkness,
Nor of the destruction *that* lays waste at noonday.

⁷ A thousand may fall at your side,
And ten thousand at your right hand;
But it shall not come near you.
⁸ Only with your eyes shall you look,
And see the reward of the wicked.

⁹ Because you have made the LORD, *who is* my refuge,
Even the Most High, your dwelling place,
¹⁰ No evil shall befall you,
Nor shall any plague come near your dwelling;
¹¹ For He shall give His angels charge over you,
To keep you in all your ways.
¹² In *their* hands they shall bear you up,
Lest you dash your foot against a stone.
¹³ You shall tread upon the lion and the cobra,
The young lion and the serpent you shall trample underfoot.

¹⁴ "Because he has set his love upon Me, therefore I will deliver him;
I will set him on high, because he has known My name.
¹⁵ He shall call upon Me, and I will answer him;
I *will be* with him in trouble;
I will deliver him and honor him.
¹⁶ With long life I will satisfy him,
And show him My salvation."

Proverbs 13:12

Hope deferred makes the heart sick,
But *when* the desire comes,
it is a tree of life.

8

Hopelessness: Opens the Door to the Enemy

In the last chapter I talked about Brice learning to overcome. He was young, and we had won the victory, but the "enemy of our souls" did not give up.

I believe, as many mothers do, that my son had a calling from God on his life. He really loved Jesus and was very sensitive to spiritual things. But he was still a normal boy. He loved his friends. He wanted to fit in, to be accepted by them.

When Brice was 10, I went up to say good night to him as I usually did. We would always talk about everything he did that day. He'd always been able to communicate his feelings, which was good.

It was October. He was lying in bed with the covers up over his head. I could hear him sniffling and crying. That was unusual; he was a happy child. I sat down on the bed, and asked, "Brice, is anything wrong?"

He didn't respond. Not a word. I asked him several times, but he wouldn't say a word and wouldn't remove the blanket.

This was extremely odd behavior for him, but I thought maybe he needed some time alone. I said, "If you want to talk, call me. I'll come up. I love you." No response.

I went downstairs expecting him to follow me, but he didn't. The next morning I heard a loud thump over my head. His room was right above ours. I ran upstairs. He was standing in the middle of the room holding his throat. He was choking and couldn't get his breath. Then he vomited across the room like a fountain.

He hadn't been sick or acted like he was coming down with anything. He just hadn't talked to me the night before. I slept with him that night and for the next two weeks. The same pattern kept occurring. He would jump up from a sound sleep and act like he was choking and vomit across the room. I put a bucket at his bedside, but it was of no use.

Two weeks of this was very stressful. You can imagine every night! I could never leave him alone. David and I were both afraid and couldn't imagine what was wrong. He had no fever. His stomach didn't hurt. He would just suddenly feel like he was choking and throw up.

I took him to the doctor, but they didn't find anything wrong and had no ideas. They gave us some sort of medicine for 10 days, but it didn't help.

One day he threw up on the way to school. We had to go back and change clothes. He was so embarrassed. I assured him it was okay, and we would get through this.

He threw up several times at school. Needless to say, we were in a quandary.

Some of the kids started making fun of him. Back then it wasn't like the bullying we see today. They were just laughing and making references to throwing up all the time. Children can sometimes find the smallest differences to belittle someone else.

Brice started not wanting to go to school. There was always this lingering fear that he might throw up. There was no warning.

During this same time in October, a friend of mine and I were asked to visit a boy from another state in the hospital after his heart surgery. He was fine when he went into the surgery, but afterward, he couldn't speak and was drawn up in a fetal position and drooled all the time. It was a pitiful situation.

Abstain From Every Appearance of Evil

My friend and I would go, take snacks and pray with the parents. It was around Halloween and it made me sad to walk the halls of these sick and dying people in every room with black cats, witches and Halloween decorations on every door and nurse's station. The Bible says to "abstain from every appearance of evil" (I Thessalonians 5:22 KJV). People act like paranormal books, movies and vampires and Halloween celebrations are fun and normal. According to the Word we should have nothing to do with these things. They have an appearance of evil. It's not just fun entertainment—that's the devil's lie. But people have to decide for themselves.

This family was crying out for help. We visited several times. The young man was 17. Sometimes they would bring him down to the lobby just to get him out of his room. We would meet them there and talk and pray with them. They were there for months.

I noticed that Brice would sit and talk to this boy like he believed he could understand. I believe the boy did understand, but he would just drool, look around and make noises. Brice was 10 and had great compassion for him.

Once I looked over at them, no one else was looking. The young man had drooled down his face and onto his shirt. Brice quietly got a tissue and wiped his face for him. It was a normal response for him. Then he just started chatting away again.

At this point Brice was still throwing up and we had no solution to the problem.

We were going into November when I asked Brice if he would like for me take him out of school to go to a Bible Study with me. A wonderful godly man, Bill French, taught the study. I had heard him many times and had great respect for him. I said, "Maybe he'll have time to pray for you."

Brice said, "Great!" So I took him out of school and wrote on the check-out form: *appointment*. It was an appointment. An appointment with God and Brice's destiny.

We got to the study and after the lesson, Bill came over to us. He was probably surprised to see a child there. He said, "How are you doing, young man?"

"Okay," Brice responded. Then Bill asked if he made straight A's.

"Nope," Brice said. "A's, B's and C's"

Then Bill did a strange thing. He started talking about hopelessness. It was really odd. Neither Brice nor I had mentioned it. It wasn't part of Bill's teaching that day. I hadn't even been thinking about it. We hadn't yet had a chance to tell Bill why we were there.

Hopelessness

Bill said when people allow hopelessness to come in and bother them it gives the enemy an open door to step right in and harass them and cause problems. Hopelessness is fear, and fear is a lack of faith.

He talked to us a few minutes and left to talk to someone else. I was disappointed because I had wanted him to pray for Brice. That didn't happen. What I didn't know was that our little conversation had already begun to set Brice free!

Brice had never told me why, over a month before, he had been crying under the blanket. I think he forgot to talk about it with everything else that was going on in life in those weeks.

We got in the car and Brice said, "That's it! That night I was crying, I was sad because my friends were treating me mean. They were leaving me out. I cried and cried. I felt so hopeless. I know it now. I had deep hopelessness and went to sleep. The enemy had an open door. He came in and slammed me. That's when I started choking and threw up."

I was shocked. "I think you're right."

Then Brice started telling me about a teacher at school who always seemed hopeless. "We need to tell her about this," he said. I thought it was kind of odd and humorous that he would suddenly recognize that about this teacher. But I knew it was true. God must have truly shown it to him.

Secret Things Belong to Us

Brice never threw up because of this again. I realized that just recognizing the tactics of the devil this time had set him free.

This new revelation would help him greatly in years to come. Again, he was an overcomer.

In the years as he grew, the truths of God revealed to him were life to him. God reveals His secrets, His heart, to us and then we have to walk them out here on earth.

> **Deuteronomy 29:29 (KJV)** The secret things belong unto the LORD our God: but those things which are revealed belong unto us and to our children for ever...

What God reveals to us, when put into practice, causes us to overcome and no man can take that revelation from us unless we let them.

> **Proverbs 13:12** Hope deferred makes the heart sick, but *when* the desire comes, *it is* a tree of life.

Isaiah 59:21 KJV

As for me, this is my covenant with them,
saith the LORD; My spirit that is upon thee,
and my words which I have put in thy
mouth, shall not depart out of thy mouth, nor
out of the mouth of thy seed, nor out of the
mouth of thy seed's seed, saith the LORD,
from henceforth and for ever.

9

A Bull to Ram Down Walls for the Kingdom

I have not seen a family yet that has escaped trials of one kind or another. Our family had survived some great spiritual battles. On the surface ours may not have seemed spiritual, but they were. The Bible says we don't war against flesh and blood (Ephesians 6:12). It also says we fight against the world and our own fleshly desires (Galatians 5:19-21).

I feel like the battle over Corey's life started at his birth. He was born two weeks late according to the doctors. I was in labor 34 hours and his heart rate dropped. I was thrilled when he finally arrived and was perfectly fine.

He was so precious to us and the cutest baby I'd ever seen! Before he reached the ripe old age of two, he displayed—I will call them—independent qualities. He knew exactly what he wanted and didn't give up easily on those desires. People now call that a "strong willed child." I wish I had known from the beginning that much of his strong willed personality was leadership. He was stretching at every age to be stronger and more independent. And he was stretching us.

Even though I had taught school, I had no training to deal with such an independent child. It was different than when I'd had them in the classroom. I could talk to the parents, pray for them, get advice from other teachers and the principal or send them home. David and I were not prepared to have one fighting us 24-7.

If I could have seen the future and known all the ways God was going to use Corey for His purposes, we would have been much more understanding. We would have prayed a lot more together instead of whining about his behavior to each other, to our friends and to God. The whining didn't do any of us much good.

Corey became a missionary in China and now he pastors a church outside Raleigh, North Carolina. When I see all he's been through, I know why God made him to be strong and forceful in his ways. But when he was little, we had no idea the course he was to take.

Not long ago he asked me to write down for him and his wife the way I had prayed for him when he was young. He had heard the stories of how we prayed, but now Corey has four wonderful children of his own, he wanted to see it more clearly.

When Corey was 12, the teenage years crashed into our lives. He wanted to date, which we flatly said no to. He could not understand. When he turned 13, I was in that dark desperate place again where I needed God's intervention. This time with Corey. I started crying out to God. He gave me a revelation of truth about the relationship between me and Corey that changed the way I prayed for him and others.

I am including part of the letter I wrote to Corey here, and I pray it will cause you to come out of agreement with how you feel and what you see with your children in the natural and come into agreement with what God says about them.

Corey's Letter

Yes, Corey, I was desperate and at the end of all natural resources I knew. I had been a teacher, but nothing prepared me for a teenager who was angry a lot of the time. Most of that anger was toward me.

I wanted desperately to help you. Dad and I were frustrated. You were more frustrated than we were!

You were smart and had huge leadership giftings. I would even say now that you had a pioneering gifting. You weren't moved by any limitations. You excelled in sports and made excellent grades. You had a mind that believed you could learn anything, which really helped you later in life.

We had tried as parents not to break your will. We wanted you to learn self-control, a gift of the spirit. We wanted you to learn to walk in love and to be kind.

Even with a rebellious attitude and actions, we purposefully never told you, you were bad…

I've heard parents say that to their kids to their face in public, "You are just bad children." Well, their actions may have been bad, but the child is not bad. If children keep hearing with their own ears, from their parents and others that they are bad, they might begin to believe it and act in bad ways. Thus it becomes a self-fulfilling prophecy.

Parents don't think it is cursing their children when they say these things. They might think "it's just conversation," "Just joking," or "just frustration talking." For example, "My daughter will always be heavy. It runs in the family." "My son can't do anything right." "My children are always fighting." "If I have a baby, it will probably have difficulty learning because one of my relatives did."

Are these statements biblical? It may look like "reality," but to keep from cursing your children, find a scripture that speaks to your case. "My children have the mind of Christ. They can learn anything." "My daughter can do all things through Christ who strengthens her. She knows how to eat right and have a balanced life. She will not live in fear of being fat."

Oh, so many awful things people say about their children, to the children and to other people.

You might be thinking, "Well, I just want to be honest and tell the truth." So, look at the truth and tell your children what it is: "You are precious to me." "I am proud of you." "You are beautiful." "No one can do this like you do." "I like the way your hair looks." "You are such a blessing in our family." If you can't say things like this, say something positive. Not just once, but all the time. Ask the Lord to change your speech about them. It will change them.

Back to Corey's Letter

...I know situations can look bleak in both your lives. It did in my situation. I understand.

On Sunday, October 2, 1990—I remember the date because I wrote it next to a verse in my Bible, you were 14 at the time—I let the family sleep in instead of "dragging" them out of bed as usual for church.

I was so sad that day. It had been a hard week with you, Corey. It seemed to be getting harder. I took my Bible out on the porch, sat in the swing and cried. I prayed the same hopeless, desperate prayers again.

I decided to just open my Bible, sometimes we do that just looking for a comforting verse, and I hoped it wouldn't be "and destruction came upon the land" or something similar.

In front of me was Psalm 42:5. I wrote your name by it and the date. It says, "Why are you cast down, O my soul? And *why* are you disquieted within me? Hope in God, for I shall yet praise Him *For* the help of His countenance.

I felt like a cartoon light bulb went off over my head. I had been in fear for you. Fear I couldn't handle you, fear for your future, fear your attitude wouldn't change, fear things would always be this way. I repented right then. I had known better, but the enemy had deceived me into thinking the battle was all mine. I had to do it right, handle it all right, respond right. It was a tormenting fear.

I read those verses over and over. I asked the Lord to help me and I received a new resolve not to let fear overcome me again and not to give up.

I went back to the way I had prayed God's Word over myself when I was healed years before. It was the same Word. The Word is God Himself, written down. I knew it and again began to apply it when I prayed for you. The Bible is His promises to us and for us so we can live that abundant overcoming life in every area…

I prayed for Corey the same way I prayed for friends, finances, and relationships. People ask "what is the will of God? How do you know His will?"

God's will is His Word!

If someone is sick, pray the Word back to God; it is His will. He wants to uphold it. He wants us to believe He's telling the truth. There is great power in the Word. The Bible says, He "uphold(s) all things by the word of His power" (Hebrews 1:3b). That is a lot of power!

God did have great things ahead for Corey. Greater than I could have imagined! All I was looking at was the natural realm. I often went back to Proverbs 4:20-23, the verses I saw when I was sick. This caused me to "attend" the Word again.

Proverbs 4:20-23
²⁰ My son, give attention to my words;
Incline your ear to my sayings.
²¹ Do not let them depart from your eyes;
Keep them in the midst of your heart;
²² For they *are* life to those who find them,
And health to all their flesh.
²³ Keep your heart with all diligence,
For out of it *spring* the issues of life.
²⁴ Put away from you a deceitful mouth,
And put perverse lips far from you.

I began a new journey with Corey. He had no idea, and if I had told him at the time, he wouldn't have listened or understood.

Attend the Word

Once again, it was me and God. I was agreeing with God again. David and I agreed but he was in a different place spiritually and very busy with work. Again, I say, God is just waiting for us to agree with what He has said.

…From that day to this day, I often pray like this for you. "Lord, I thank you that Corey attends to your Word. He hungers and thirsts after You. He hears Your voice, Lord, and a stranger's voice he will not follow. He is taught the Word of the Lord and great will be his peace and the peace of his children. He walks in Your ways, Father. He has the mind of Christ." And other verses.

Sometimes I'd pray all of them; sometimes I'd just pray one. Many times when we were arguing, I'd go in the bathroom (a good secret place) and pray. "Lord, I don't care what I see. I don't care what I hear. Corey is a godly man. He loves You. He loves his family. He hungers after You. Sometimes I'd cry and say, "I don't care how I feel, Lord, or how many tears I cry, Your Word is true and not what I see! (They don't call that the "throne" for no reason. God on His throne has heard me many times from my bathroom, and He has answered me there.)

I wish I had started praying that way when you were younger, but God uses all things in our lives for His glory. I wasn't whining anymore, or asking why. I did whatever I thought I should do. Answered you in whatever way I was led, but I kept the Word of God in my mouth. I kept my confessions about you pure…

The High Priest of Our Confession

I would love to say I saw an immediate turn around in Corey's life, but it was about four years until we actually saw changes in him. All the while, he was going to Christian school and youth group every week. I am sure God used teachers, youth leaders, even acquaintances as I diligently prayed. But the Word was the main force in his life.

God says in Jeremiah 1:12(ASV), "I am watching over my Word to perform it." When I would feel weak or see something contrary to my prayers, I would cast down every imagination that would come up against my mind (II Corinthians 10:5).

Cast Down

> **Isaiah 59:21b**...My words which I have put in your mouth, shall not depart from your mouth, nor from the mouth of your descendants, nor from the mouth of your descendants' descendants," says the LORD, "from this time and forevermore."

Now this scripture, which came out of God's mouth, is talking about *me, my* children and *my* grandchildren! The devil would say to me the same tired phrase, "What if..." Again! I would cast that thought down and say, "NO! Corey hungers and thirsts after righteousness!" That *what if* statement was a trap of Satan to get me into fear.

I can't say I never felt sad or tired, but I decided to act like the cartoon dog with a bone. I was hanging onto the Word. No matter what. It was his *life*. He had been entrusted to us by God.

I heard a TV preacher tell a story while I was praying for

Corey. He said he had been pretty wild when he was young. He got saved and God called him into ministry. One day he decided he was tired of struggling in the ministry and begged God to let him go. He wanted to go back to the way it was. It was easier. He heard God say, "I can't let you go, son, because your mother is ever before my face."

When I heard that, it was like a shot in the arm. I thought, "I can do that. I can be before God's face. Surely for this one I love so much, I can ever be before God's face. I will never give up."

Romans 4:17 says Abraham called things that are not, as though they were. If God said Abraham was the father of many nations, Abraham said he was the father of many nations. He said it even though he was old and Sarah was old and her womb was dead, he said he was the father of many nations.

He spoke it out, and Isaac was born.

That's what I did. I spoke His Word in faith, out loud if I could, under my breath when I couldn't. I wanted to hear it. I wanted God to hear it. I wanted the enemy to hear it. I didn't give the enemy any ground. I would not speak in fear or hopelessness.

Self-pity is a Pit

Most of my life I had lived in fear or self-pity. I did not see a lot of fruit from praying in those years. Self-pity is a pit and I was in it a lot. Not just over the big things in life, but even for little things that did not go my way.

One morning, years ago, before I woke up, the Lord spoke to me and said, "You are in self-pity again." My eyes popped open, "Really?" I asked. I had not even recognized it. So I repented. That's what we do. We repent and go on. There is not a "mourning period" required. He has already forgiven us. He forgave us and it was all covered when we accepted Him as our Savior. So when a new sin crops up in life, recognize it, repent and go on and do right.

> **I John 1:9** If we confess our sins, He is faithful and just to forgive us *our* sins and to cleanse us from all unrighteousness.

When you've done what He instructs us, then ask the Lord to help you in any area, like self-pity, so you won't fall in again. We know when we sin. The Holy Spirit who lives in us will show us. God won't always wake you up from sleep, but He has ways of showing us, because He loves us.

Agreement

During Corey's teen years I learned a lot about the power of agreement.

> **Matthew 18:19 (KJV)** Again I say unto you, that if two of you shall agree on earth as touching any thing that they shall ask, it shall be done for them of my Father which is in heaven.

I mostly just agreed with God back then. Be sure if you are agreeing with someone and you know it is God's will, that neither of you uproot your answer by speaking against the truths you've prayed. For example, if you've prayed for someone sick with cancer to be healed, don't turn around and say, "I sure hope they get better. People with this kind of cancer don't usually make it." Another example is, "I've prayed for my marriage, but it's not going to make it." In these so-called "reality" statements, you are coming out of faith and confessing the opposite of what you've prayed.

83

Now, David and I agree on many things in our lives, for his job, our children, other people. God was so gracious to help us during these years. He is the One who helped us stand.

Expect Miracles

I will never let go of the truth that God honors His Word. He cannot lie.

> **Numbers 23:19** God is not a man, that he should lie; neither the son of man, that he should repent: hath he said, and shall he not do it? or hath he spoken, and shall he not make it good?

When I don't know how to pray, I declare the Word...then expect miracles. I feel like God is just waiting for someone to expect miracles.

I watched a movie the other day. At the end it showed a skyline view of New York City. The commentator said, "People here pray for miracles every day...sometimes they get to see one." I thought that was kind of sad. People are praying for miracles every day. How many expect to see one?

Back to Corey's letter

> When you were a junior in high school we started seeing changes in your behavior. You started asking questions like you never had before about spiritual things. You became a Christian at age 3½, but we had not seen much evidence of salvation. I knew you were a

Christian because you really wanted Jesus to be your Savior. You came as a little child.

One day during your junior year at Auburn University you came home to have lunch and talk. I was thrilled of course. As we drove down the road—I remember exactly where we were when this question came up. You said, "Hey mom, what's wrong with me? All my friends are Christians, but they are satisfied to read the Bible 10 or 15 minutes a day. I want to read it all the time. It's like that verse, 'You hunger and thirst after righteousness.'"

I was stunned!!

I had never told you I prayed that verse over you almost every day. I told you then. You were pretty shocked, like someone had slapped you. We both got excited! It had been six years since I'd started praying the Word. I had started speaking truth and life over you when you were in 9th grade. It had given me a lot of peace during those years. I wasn't praying out of my intellect or understanding. I was praying and decreeing truth.

We saw great changes in Corey that year and in his senior year. He became very involved with a campus Christian organization. His heart was being pulled towards missions. He told me about being in a meeting where the speaker said there were 244 churches in the Auburn area. The large city in China that Corey would be moving to after college only had two. Four days after he graduated from college, he left for China as a missionary.

He loved China, and still does. He was there for five years.

Currently, Corey pastors a multi-cultural church in Morrisville, North Carolina. He is married and has four children.

One day when Corey was still at Auburn, David and I sat down with a friend of ours who believes like we do, that God still speaks today. This man has a prophetic gift like the Bible talks about in I Corinthians 12:28. He started praying for Corey.

He had never met him and Corey wasn't there. He said, "Corey is like a bull. He will ram down walls for the Kingdom of God."

The words God gave our friend have been so true. Ever since Corey was young, he wanted to press ahead, push the limits. He has come through many struggles. Now he presses and pushes the limits for the glory and Kingdom of God!

Matthew 18:19 b KJV

If two of you shall agree on earth as
touching any thing that they shall ask, it
shall be done for them of my Father which is
in heaven.

10

THE PRAYER OF AGREEMENT
IS A STRONG PRAYER

Much of my and David's earlier years together were plagued with financial problems. He had a good job right out of college with an accounting firm, and I taught school, yet we always seemed to struggle with paying our bills and having any money left over. There was no money for fun and no money to save.

I used to whine (I was good at that) to my friends and they whined back at me about their finances. I told a Bible study teacher one time that David wouldn't even give me a dollar. Talk about self-pity. And my statement wasn't even true!

David was an accountant; financial stresses bothered him more because he was gifted in the area of finance and administration, but it wasn't working in our personal lives.

During these years though, I had seen miracles of healing, I'd been delivered of demonic oppression, yet I didn't even think about believing for God to give us more than enough in our finances. Abundance looked impossible.

In 1993, Brice was in junior high, Corey in high school.

David and I had many discussions, as most couples do, on finances, and cutting our spending, saving some. He was always down about it. I wasn't very helpful.

I was really thinking about teaching again. I had taught elementary school for 2½ years before Corey was born. Afterward, we decided I should be a stay-at-home mom. I loved every minute of it, but my boys were older now, and I could work. We talked about it and we prayed about it.

There was something deep inside me that told me I needed to be at home with Brice when he arrived from school. He wasn't a little boy anymore, but I had a nagging feeling it was necessary for me to be there if he needed to talk.

David was fine with me going to work. His mother had worked most of his growing up years. My mother had worked and both of our sisters had worked. He wasn't set on my working though, so we just prayed.

During this time I had a sweet friend that prayed with me every week. She had two daughters who were older than my sons. They were in college. She and her husband were going through the same financial crunch we were. She was seeking God about their future and whether she should look for a job or not. It wasn't that we were lazy. We just wanted what God wanted—whatever that was—and when we found that path, we knew we would be at peace about the decision.

Where Two or More Agree

One Friday, I came across a scripture that I'd read many times. I had even prayed and declared it, for healing in my body. I had also prayed it for my children. Only this time when I read it, it was new to me again.

Matthew 18:19 KJV Again I say unto you, That if two of you shall agree on earth as touching any thing that they shall ask, it shall be done for them of my Father which is in heaven.

Even though I knew God wanted us to have an abundant life, I thought, *Is this really true, even for finances? Can two or more agree for financial blessings?*

I got so excited I ran to the phone to call Betty. We had prayed about our children, our marriages, even our finances, but we'd never prayed we would be prosperous and we'd never agreed with God, if it was ok with Him, that we wouldn't have to go to work.

I was back in new territory, exploring God's kingdom promises again. I didn't know anyone who believed that two could agree on financial provision. We all prayed about it, worried about it, discussed it. Here I stood on the edge of the cliff of believing again. I was excited because God's Spirit in me was preparing my mind and heart to believe for something that I had not thought possible.

On the phone with Betty I said, "You know the scripture, Matthew 18:19?"

"Yes," she said.

"Well, is it really true?" I asked. "Can two agree on *any*thing, really agree, and it will be done?" I could tell through the phone that she was getting excited. "Can you and I agree that we won't have to go back to work if its ok with God and that He will bring in financial provision and blessings that we need?"

She said, "I think we can."

I said, "I'll be right over." Something began stirring and burning in me again as I stood on the edge of this revelation. The truth of God's Word was starting to be life to me in the area of finances. I didn't know it, but God was about to show us, again, that He was a miracle working God.

We could have agreed on the phone, but I felt this was serious. We had to be face to face. We were agreeing, totally, and not coming out of agreement.

So I went in and sat on her sofa. We discussed agreement on the Word, and decided on our agreement. We agreed that we would be able to stay at home to be with our children and be available when they needed us. We also agreed for abundance in finances.

Foundations of Tithing and Blessing Israel

Now, we did have most of our foundation in order. Both she and her husband (whose name is also David) tithed, and so did we. We had tithed for years. We also gave above our tithes.

> **Malachi 3:10-12 NIV** Bring the whole tithe into the storehouse, that there may be food in my house. **Test me** in this," says the LORD Almighty, "and **see if I** will not throw open the floodgates of heaven and pour out so much blessing that there will not be room enough to store it. [11] I will prevent pests from devouring your crops, and the vines in your fields will not drop their fruit before it is ripe," says the LORD Almighty. [12] "Then all the nations will call you blessed, for yours will be a delightful land," says the LORD Almighty.

Betty's family and our family also loved and blessed Israel. We did these things because the Bible said to, not to get anything, but because the Bible says when you do these things, you will be blessed.

Genesis 12:3 "I will bless those who bless you (Israel), And I will curse him who curses you; And in you all the families of the earth shall be blessed."

Now that Betty and I were beginning to believe the whole truth about agreement, we were in a new posture to receive from God.

Posture to Receive

Betty and I agreed that Friday. We just said, "Lord, according to this verse in your Word, You said if we agree on anything it will be done. So we agree that our husbands will make enough money, or finances will come from other sources, so we can stay home. It is the desire of our hearts and we delight ourselves in You, Lord."

Well, there was no great lightning and thunder show, no trumpet from heaven affirming our declaration of agreement. But we knew something was different. Now I had a friend who truly agreed with me, and we would not be moved off our agreement with each other and God, until we saw the fruit of our prayers.

Neither of us told our Davids about it, because it was a precious thing to us. A new treasure. We didn't want anyone making light of our agreement. So we prayed together every week for months and thanked the Lord that His Word was true.

Hebrews 11:6 But without faith *it is* impossible to please *Him,* for he who comes to God must believe that He is, and *that* He is a rewarder of those who diligently seek Him.

I didn't know at the time, what a bad financial state we were in. I knew things were really tight and that David was a little quieter than usual.

Over the next few months, Betty and I found other scriptures about financial prosperity and blessing. We started praying these together, back to the Lord. We also prayed them each day individually.

In the same way that the Word was life to me when I was healed and praying for my children, it was life to me now in the financial realm. No matter what my bank account or the economy showed, we kept speaking truth and believing that we were prospering.

Currently, there are many teachings and books on the subject of finances and God's provision, but we had never heard of or read any of them. We just got desperate and hung onto that one verse and then the others we found. We began to know in our hearts, not just our minds, that we were blessed to be a blessing. Our faith-man inside was growing stronger. "Faith comes by hearing and hearing by the Word of God" (Romans 10:17). I was hearing the Word over and over on God's ways and His desire to bless us and I believed it.

Keep the Word in Your Mouth

This was in August of 1993. I prayed diligently, sometimes twice a day. It's not that God doesn't know His own Word, He said to "put the Word in my mouth" and believe (Isaiah 51:16). That's what I was doing. I kept the Word before my eyes until it was deeply rooted in my heart.

It was sometime in October that I told David about what Betty and I had learned about agreement with each other and God's Word. I told him we were believing for financial abundance. He didn't laugh or make light of it. He said, "Did you know that the Friday you and Betty first prayed I was walking around the streets of a North Carolina town on my business trip, crying out to God? I was desperate, asking Him what I should do!"

I had had no idea! David encouraged me to keep it up, and I did.

I quit saying we didn't have any money. I quit saying we can't afford anything. I quit dwelling on negative reports. I kept the Word in my mouth. I said, "Our barns are filled with plenty and our vats burst forth with new wine" (Proverbs 3:9-10).

I said, "The windows of heaven are open over us and blessings are being poured on us that we don't have room enough to receive" (Malachi 3:10).

I said, "We have no lack and we shall not want" (Proverbs 31:11 & Psalm 23:1).

I said, "The Lord supplies all our needs according to His riches in glory by Christ Jesus" (Philippians 4:19).

Blessing and Position

Just as before when my body was healed, we saw a great change in David's position. He was promoted to right under the head of the company and received a $1000 raise per month. That was the manifested answer to our months of praying the Word, God's truth, back to Him. God honors His Word.

We saw more changes gradually. Betty and David became totally debt free. We were both able to give more. We love to give. I know God has given us the gift of giving and we were able to give way above our tithe, to the poor, to help people pay their bills and to give to ministries in Africa and other parts of the world.

I've heard several teachers ask, "If you don't have enough, how are you going to help anybody else in need?"

Our lives were again changed as we saw another miracle unfold before our eyes.

That's not the end of course. We believe the blessing and favor of God surrounds us as a shield because we trust in Him.

> **Psalm 5:12** For You, O LORD, will bless the righteous; With favor You will surround him as *with* a shield.

I guess it sounds a little strange to some people, but we expect God's blessing to come upon us and overtake us in every way. We don't sit around bemoaning the times and the economy. God's economy has no deficit, so we just praise Him for His abundant blessing. He "daily loads us with His benefits."

> **Psalm 68:19** Blessed *be* the Lord,
> *Who* daily loads us *with benefits,*
> The God of our salvation! Selah

So we decided to believe and not doubt—it is definitely a decision. Sometimes it seemed all the forces of evil tried to move us off this path we had planted our feet on. Our path was to believe no matter what came. We would stand and not give up.

I heard someone ask "If you go back, what do you go back to? Believing that God wants you poor and needy? That God doesn't bless so we can be a blessing?"

That old thinking is contrary to everything in the Bible and all we know of the character of our God. The Bible is a book that reveals God's heart on many things. One position it holds is that God is a God who blesses His people. He is lavish. He is not stingy. He does not want us to eke out a little here and a little there, so we can barely make it.

Thinking contrary to the Word is believing a lie of the enemy. Even a lot of people in the Church believe wrongly. There seems to be a commonly held belief that if you are poor and still faithful to the Church and God that you are more humble.

God says "goodness and mercy follow me all the days of my life" (Psalm 23:6), and He came to "give us life more abundant" (John 10:10), that He will pour out blessing upon us so that we don't have room enough to receive it (Malachi 3:10). That's a lot of blessing! That's His plan for us!

The prayer of agreement is a strong prayer. It is the Word, and the Bible says the Word is alive (Hebrews 4:12), and that the Word accomplished what it was sent to do. (Isaiah 55:11).

I am including the verses Betty and I agreed on for blessing and prosperity. If you can agree on one verse, there is life in that one verse. One single Word of God can change your life and circumstances forever.

May you see the goodness of God in the land of the Living (Psalm 27:13).

Scriptures to Prosper in Abundance

Joshua 1:8 This Book of the Law shall not depart from your mouth, but you shall meditate in it day and night, that you may observe to do according to all that is written in it. For then you will make your way prosperous, and then you will have good success.

Genesis 15:1 KJV After these things the word of the LORD came unto Abram in a vision, saying, Fear not, Abram: I am thy shield, and thy exceeding great reward.

Deuteronomy 7:9 AMP Know, recognize, *and* understand therefore that the Lord your God, He is God, the faithful God, Who keeps covenant and steadfast love *and* mercy with those who love Him and keep His commandments, to a thousand generations,

Deuteronomy 8:18 "And you shall remember the LORD your God, for *it is* He who gives you power to get wealth, that He may establish His covenant which He swore to your fathers, as *it is* this day.

Deuteronomy 28—whole chapter to be read

Psalm 1:3 He shall be like a tree planted by the rivers of water,
That brings forth its fruit in its season, Whose leaf also shall not wither;
And whatever he does shall prosper.

Psalm 34:10 AMP The young lions lack food and suffer hunger, but they who seek (inquire of and require) the Lord [by right of their need and on the authority of His Word], none of them shall lack any beneficial thing.

Psalm 35:27 Let them shout for joy and be glad, Who favor my righteous cause; And let them say continually, "Let the LORD be magnified, Who has pleasure in the prosperity of His servant."

Psalm 68:19 Blessed *be* the Lord, *Who* daily loads us *with benefits,* The God of our salvation! Selah

Psalm 84:11b No good *thing* will He withhold from those who walk uprightly.

Psalm 112:1-3 Blessed *is* the man *who* fears the LORD, *Who* delights greatly in His commandments. His descendants will be mighty on earth; The generation of the upright will be blessed. Wealth and riches *will be* in his house, And his righteousness endures forever.

Psalm 115:14 May the LORD give you increase more and more, you and your children.

Proverbs 10:6a Blessings *are* on the head of the righteous,

Proverbs 10:22 The blessing of the LORD makes *one* rich, And He adds no sorrow with it.

Proverbs 11:25 NIV A generous person will prosper; whoever refreshes others will be refreshed.

Proverbs 13:21b-22 NIV the righteous are rewarded with good things.[22] A good person leaves an inheritance for their children's children, but a sinner's wealth is stored up for the righteous.

Proverbs 14:11b the tent of the upright will flourish

Proverbs 14:21b NIV blessed is the one who is kind to the needy.

Proverbs 15:6 NIV The house of the righteous contains great treasure, but the income of the wicked brings ruin.

Proverbs 16:3 AMP Roll your works upon the Lord [commit and trust them wholly to Him; He will cause your thoughts to become agreeable to His will, and] so shall your plans be established *and* succeed.

Proverbs 16:7 AMP When a man's ways please the Lord, He makes even his enemies to be at peace with him.

Proverbs 19:17 NIV Whoever is kind to the poor lends to the LORD, and he will reward them for what they have done.

Proverbs 21:21 He who follows righteousness and mercy
Finds life, righteousness, and honor.

Proverbs 22:4 NLT True humility and fear of the LORD lead to riches, honor, and long life.

Proverbs 22:9 NLT Blessed are those who are generous, because they feed the poor.

Proverbs 28:8 AMP He who by charging excessive interest *and* who by unjust efforts to get gain increases his material possession gathers it for him [to spend] who is kind *and* generous to the poor

Proverbs 28:20 NLT The trustworthy person will get a rich reward,
but a person who wants quick riches will get into trouble.

Proverbs 28:27 He who gives to the poor will not lack

Ecclesiastes 2:26 NLT God gives wisdom, knowledge, and joy to those who please him. But if a sinner becomes wealthy, God takes the wealth away and gives it to those who please him.

Malachi 3:10 Bring all the tithes into the storehouse, That there may be food in My house, And try Me now in this," Says the LORD of hosts, "If I will not open for you the windows of heaven And pour out for you *such* blessing That *there will* not *be room* enough *to receive it.*

Luke 6:38 Give, and it will be given to you: good measure, pressed down, shaken together, and running over will be put into your bosom. For with the same measure that you use, it will be measured back to you."

Luke 12:31 AMP Only aim at *and* strive for *and* seek His kingdom, and all these things shall be supplied to you also.

2 Corinthians 2:14a Now thanks *be* to God who always leads us in triumph in Christ

2 Corinthians 8:9b though He was rich, yet for your sakes He became poor, that you through His poverty might become rich.

2 Corinthians 9:8 AMP And God is able to make all grace (every favor and earthly blessing) come to you in abundance, so that you may always *and* under all circumstances *and* whatever the need be self-sufficient [possessing enough to require no aid or support and furnished in abundance for every good work and charitable donation].

Galatians 3:29 And if you *are* Christ's, then you are Abraham's seed, and heirs according to the promise.

Philippians 4:19 And my God shall supply all your need according to His riches in glory by Christ Jesus.

3 John 2 Beloved, I pray that you may prosper in all things and be in health, just as your soul prospers.

2 Peter 1:4 by which have been given to us exceedingly great and precious promises, that through these you may be partakers of the divine nature, having escaped the corruption *that is* in the world through lust.

Proverbs 1:33 AMP But whoso hearkens to me [Wisdom] shall dwell securely *and* in confident trust and shall be quiet, without fear *or* dread of evil.

Ephesians 4:32

And be kind to one another, tenderhearted, forgiving one another, even as God in Christ forgave you.

11

PERFECT LAW OF LIBERTY

"You were tied together with barbed wire and now you are tied together with lace." This was a prophetic word David and I received back in the 1990's from a man who operated in a prophetic gifting. Only God could have shown him this, and have him say it in such a profound (and accurate) way.

In previous chapters I have alluded to my marriage several times as not always being blissful. Our family looked great on the outside. We were a sweet young couple with two precious boys. We were always at church. I taught Sunday school and children's church. David played on the church softball team. Every time the church doors were open, we were there.

Inside the doors of our home, things were very different.

David and I married in 1972. We were so in love. These days, David and I would both say that we had been "in love with love." We started dating in March that year and were engaged two months later. We saw each other almost every day. He quoted me poetry and we talked about the future. It was exciting to be in love.

He had the bluest eyes I'd ever seen and light blond hair. His blond hair was real, and not from the beach. He had worked for the city on a brush truck, picking up tree limbs and debris the summer before we started dating.

Absolutely smitten, we married in August that year.

The first six months of marriage, we were mostly miserable. We didn't know each other at all of course. His gorgeous blue eyes and my long brown hair and personality only went so far. Reality set in.

David was controlling and I was timid. Being the baby of my family, I had been indulged by my parents most of my life. If I wanted anything or had certain opinions and David disagreed, I was shocked. He was very verbal and I was very quiet…not in a good way.

This man I had married was a product of two hard working parents. His dad worked the day shift in a cotton mill and his mom worked nights most of his growing up years. He and his sister Charlotte became pretty independent, but never got in too much trouble. They looked after themselves and each other. David told me not long ago, that his sister signed all of his report cards. After she left home, he guessed he signed them himself. They weren't trying to hide anything; I think they were just trying not to bother their parents.

David and Charlotte made excellent grades; David even got a scholarship form the Alabama Society of CPAs for his last two years of college. Charlotte received many college honors of her own. Neither had problems in education, but their family life was rather quiet. Not much communication. I think they were very respectful to their parents. They knew their parents expected them to do well, so they did. They saw how hard they worked, so they pushed themselves to do well.

I did not spend much time in David's home before we were married, but I observed that it was different from mine. Our situation was not unusual. Most couples who marry come from different backgrounds or lifestyles.

About the only thing we had in common was that we were Baptist. We were raised for the most part in church. The rest of our separate lives were night and day.

One day, his mom and I were walking downtown and there was a sidewalk sale. She saw an overcoat on sale for $10.00. She said, "I sure would like to have one of these."

I asked, "Well, why don't you get one?"

She kept walking and said, "Oh, I don't need to spend the money."

I was floored. I knew they didn't look like they had much money. They lived very simply and frugally. But surely they could have afforded a ten-dollar coat. And they could have.

David had grown up with Christian parents who had a poverty mentality. A poverty mentality is when a person thinks he or she will never prosper financially. That life will always be the same for him and he accepts where he is. Even people who have money can be subject to a poverty mentality. They can be wealthy, but afraid they will never have enough or afraid they will lose what they have.

It wasn't David's fault and it wasn't his parents' fault. This way of thinking and living had been passed down from generation to generation. It is not unusual for people to think that way. It is all they know.

My family—while they weren't the Rockefellers—when they had money, they would spend it. My dad had no problem buying what he wanted. If I wanted something, as I got older, I usually got it. I even had a credit card for one special store while I was still in high school. That was unheard of! I didn't spend much money there, but the fact that I carried a credit card with me was awesome to me.

Needless to say, a poverty mentality was not a problem in my household, even though both my parents had come from meager circumstances in the hills of Tennessee. We had coal miners and farmers in our family and a few preachers, but my dad had dreams and he wanted his family to share in those.

Many of my dad's dreams and longings disrupted our family. We moved often. I went to seven different schools while growing up in different towns. My mom had great insecurities because of all the changes.

There was a lot of arguing and bitterness between my mom and dad most of my life. David's family may have had that too, but they never talked much. My mom and dad didn't really fight. They were discussing loudly, and mom never seemed to get her point across that she would like to settle down with three children.

Besides all that, daddy didn't really mind spending money, and that was part of the discussion too. He would trade cars, and she would wonder how she was going to buy groceries.

Silent Treatment

Not only were David and I brought up differently, we *were* different. We both thought we were right about everything. David was gruff and would blow up at me and get over whatever discussion we were having. I would stuff my opinions and not talk to him...for two or three weeks at a time. That's hard to do when you live in the same house, but I managed to do it. Now I recognize that I was trying to manipulate him into seeing my point of view, whatever that was.

We kept our struggles hidden from everyone. Counseling was not an option. People only went to counseling when they were really desperate. We did not realize how desperate we really were. We lived this way for years, so it became normal to us. Our boys never knew about our problems. We had decided before we had children we would not argue in front of them. I had heard so much arguing, I didn't want my children to live that way. We discussed issues behind closed doors. I suppose you could call it "discussing" when we talked.

What is so sad to me now is that we had both been in church all our lives. I had been a Christian since I was 14 and David since he was 10. Being a Christian and hearing sermons every Sunday will not save your marriage. It will not change your children. It will not cause you to forgive. Nothing will be different unless you take what you learn and apply it to your life.

I had taught lessons on forgiveness, and did not know how to forgive. I heard if you want a change in your life, make a change. Well, I wanted David to change, but I didn't know how to get that to happen. When we did talk, situations just seemed to get more heated. I was trying to change someone who did not know how to change, didn't think he needed to change, and didn't want to change. Life was too busy with work, two children and a pouting wife to even think about it all. I was putting all my expectation of change on him, when the one who needed to do the changing was me.

Strife Causes Confusion and Every Evil Work

After 17 years of marriage you would think that two people who loved the Lord and had two children could live in peace and harmony; not in our case.

About 23 years ago, David and I had not been speaking to each other for about three weeks. During those weeks we had even hosted a party at our house with friends from church. The guys all watched ball games and the ladies—being the "spiritual ones"—all went upstairs and prayed together. It was a lovely day, except David and I were not speaking. The strife between us was awful. No one picked up on it. No one knew. We were good at cover up.

Not long after that, I went to bed crying one night, full of self-pity (though I didn't recognize it then). I cried out loud to God, "God, David is so mean to me. The kids talk ugly to me all the time." It was pity, pity, pity. I fell asleep crying and in the middle of the night I woke up with an object—really, a tangible object—sitting on my chest. It was dark, heavy and round. I could barely see it, but I could feel it. I could hardly breathe. I tried to go back to sleep. When I woke up, the strangest thing happened. I had no voice. I mean I could not speak at all. I went to bed with a voice and woke without even a raspy sound.

I'd had laryngitis before, but it had always started with a respiratory problem. Never had I gone to bed speaking clearly and—boom—no voice the next morning.

I knew in my heart that this was a supernatural occurrence. Not in a good way. But I didn't understand it. I certainly did not relate the crying and self-pity with it.

As days went by, my voice did eventually become raspy and I developed a deep cough. Still no sinus problems though. It was baffling. It hung on for about a week.

A special speaker was coming to church to speak to our women a few weeks later. Still coughing, I made up excuses in my mind of why I couldn't and shouldn't go. But our pastor's wife really wanted us all to come. I thought I could probably sneak out early if it was boring. The only thing I knew about the speaker was that she was a Mennonite, but I didn't have Google to find out what that was in those days.

Our church was small. About 60 women had come for a two day conference. I sat quietly trying not to cough too loudly. I smiled like I was glad to be there, but I was thinking, *I could be at home doing laundry.*

When our pastor's wife introduced the speaker I was surprised. She was an older woman. She wore a long cotton dress and her hair was pulled back in a tight bun. She reminded me of Amish people I'd seen in photos.

God Sends Answers When We Need Them

She took the platform and began to speak. She had such a merry way of speaking. The joy I felt and the wisdom I heard made me forget my cough, and the laundry and all the problems I'd had 30 minutes before at home. Her speech was filled with knowledge of years of being friends with Jesus. I was a Christian of course, but I'd never seen or heard this kind of love pouring out as she spoke of God's love for us and the relationship we can have with Him. I hung on every word. It was like the love of God was splashing over all of us. I felt refreshed just sitting there.

She spoke of forgiveness like no one I'd ever heard. She gave examples of her life struggles. She told how she had had to learn to forgive when she didn't want to and how God had turned the situation around for her and blessed her. She spoke about forgiveness in such a different way, I was overcome. I realized I'd never really forgiven. Ever!

Forgiveness is the Key

We had a break after the morning session with snacks and drinks. We all went into the basement of our church. She was talking to some of the women. I went up and told her about my experience with the form sitting on my chest and now several weeks later I was still coughing. I told her I had gone to bed crying and telling God how everyone was mean to me, no one understood me.

She was very sweet, but not very sympathetic. She said, "Well, honey, you were so into self-pity that the devil had an open door. He just came right in and hit you with the problem."

I was shocked! I did not expect that reaction. Then I knew she was right. I had so much self-pity in my life I'm surprised other things didn't happen to me. God was gracious to me. Now I know that I had not only left the door wide open for the devil, but I had also thrown out a welcome mat for him to come in to kill, steal and destroy. That's what the enemy does. For Christians, the devil has no access unless we give it to him

In my own family growing up and in David's family, I could plainly see the inroads the devil took to destroy peace. He uses every avenue to suppress and deceive.

The Bible says God gives us authority to trample on scorpions and demons.

> **Luke 10:19** Behold, I give you the authority to trample on serpents and scorpions, and over all the power of the enemy, and nothing shall by any means hurt you.

All of the enemy's tactics are under our feet, but we have to know it and believe it! If we open the door and lay out a welcome mat for him through doubt and unbelief, self-pity, fear, unforgiveness, strife, etc., he just walks in like he owns the place. Then he tries to torment, harass and kill God's people.

Close the Door

I had no idea! I did not know about spiritual warfare. I had experienced the enemy's darts and lies most of my life, but I thought it was just me, personalities, or just people. I never would have considered it was the devil.

Back to the afternoon session, the ladies were each given paper to write down the names of the people we needed to forgive. The red paper symbolized the blood of Jesus. We crumpled the paper into a little ball and threw it into a basket that was passed around.

Matilda, our speaker, told us that as we threw our papers away we should pray and forgive the people whose names we had written. We were to tell the Lord, "I forgive them and give them a new start, a clean slate, as if they'd never hurt me." We were supposed to do this as an act of our will, because our emotions might not want to agree.

This kind of forgiveness is what Jesus did for us. He gave us a clean slate when we received what He did for us on the cross. The Bible says, He washes away our sin (Acts 22:16). It reminds me of the seashore: the little rocks, shells and debris caught on the sand, but then the waves wash in and wash out, leaving the shore all white and clean. So when we believe He did that for us and receive it as our own, in that moment we are brand new. No sin. Wow!

An Act of Your Will

So could I do that for David? Could I give him a new slate as if he'd never hurt me after 17 years of marriage? Could I forgive all the bickering and cross words and hurts? I knew I had to. I wanted to, but I hesitated. Matilda said to do it as an act of your will, you may not feel it. You probably won't. But say, "I forgive _____ and give them a new start, a clean slate right now, as if they'd never hurt me." Then she said, "Now you need to bless them. As much as you can, ask God to bless them."

Matilda talked to us about a law in the Bible called "the Perfect Law of Liberty." I had never seen it in my whole life.

> **James 1:25** But he who looks into the perfect law of liberty and continues *in it,* and is not a forgetful hearer but a doer of the work, this one will be blessed in what he does.

111

Recently I was able to contact Matilda after 20 years. It was a miracle that I found her. I guess I can thank God for certain aspects of the Internet. She sounded exactly the same at age 85: full of joy and overflowing with the love of Jesus. I thought, *Oh God, I want to be that joyful letting your love flow out of me at 85!*

I asked her if I could use some quotes from a book she wrote that David and I read over and over. In the book she describes forgiving and blessing those who hurt you. Her book is called *Leap for Joy*, and I told her that I did not think I could explain the Perfect Law of Liberty as well as she did in her book. She gave me her blessing and permission. I am so grateful for her obedience in forgiving and teaching people all over the world about forgiving. She says she still uses the same principles today that the Lord taught her all those years ago.

EXCERPTS FROM *LEAP FOR JOY*
by Matilda Kipfer
(Scripture quoted is King James Version)

The Perfect Law of Liberty

The Lord spoke to me that morning and said, "Matilda, if you are going to be involved in My ministry, then you are going to have to understand how to operate my laws." Now, God does not have two sets of laws, one in heaven that He operates on His throne and then another set of laws He operates from His kingdom within us. No! No! The same laws God uses there, He uses here. There is no division in God. God the Father, God the Son, and God the Holy

Spirit are one. They operate as one. So God said to me, "Matilda, you need to understand my laws."

As I meditated that day, and in the days to follow, God began to open up to me the principles of His perfect law—the Law of Liberty.

The purpose of Jesus coming to this earth was to save, redeem, restore, heal, and make whole. This was the total ministry of Jesus. It always has been, and always will be, because Jesus is the same yesterday, today and forever. Again, I say, it is to save, redeem, restore, heal, and make whole. This is what He does in my life day after day. Every day He is working down in me His salvation, His redemption, His restoration, His healing, His wholeness to the world. Through us is now the only way He has to get His ministry into the earth. I know now that God wants to save, redeem, restore, heal and make whole my husband, my children and my grandchildren. He wants to take me into my church and administer His ministry to my pastor, my friends, and fellow members. He wants His ministry to flow out from me to all I come in contact with.

If we now recognize it is our job to serve to our generation the ministry of Jesus, there is something we have to know that is so basic. It is James 2:8, and it is called the royal law. *"If ye fulfill the royal law according to the scripture, thou shalt love they neighbor as thyself, ye do well."* Galatians 5:14 says, *"For all the law is fulfilled in one word, even this: thou shalt love thy neighbor as thyself."* In these verses we are commanded to love our neighbor. But the only way I can properly love my neighbor is when I begin to understand that Jesus is my self-worth. Therefore, I have respect for myself first of all, and then I am able to respect and enjoy you.

In James 1:25 it is called a *"perfect law of liberty,"* *"But whoso looketh into the perfect law of liberty, and continueth therein, he being a doer of the work, this man shall be blessed in his deed."* Blessings are ours when we continue in the perfect law, that is, loving our neighbor as ourselves.

This is the perfect law that Jesus operated on the cross. When He said, *"Father, forgive them, for they know not what they do."* (Luke 23:24). He released a law on earth that was so powerful that hell was shaken. He released an open door. He released a way of escape, and 3,000 of the people who put Him to death, got saved on the day of Pentecost, and daily people were added to the Church. That law was so powerful that it forgave me of all my sins. Not 99.9%, but all.

If we are going to be involved in the ministry of Jesus, it must be a ministry of new beginnings. Jesus gave me a brand new beginning when He bore my sins on the cross. He bore everything I have ever done and any hurts I have ever had. He didn't live out of His hurt. When we hang on to our hurts, in essence we are saying, "Jesus, for this portion, I really don't believe You died."

That law was so powerful that it forgave me of all my sins and transgressions. Now I stand before God just as though I had never sinned. It removed my sins as far as the East is from the West. God took them and buried them in the deepest sea. That law was so powerful that it put my name in the Lamb's Book of Life. That law was so powerful that I, who deserved to go to hell, will now spend eternity forever and ever in heaven. This is God's royal law in operation toward me.

How to Operate
The Perfect Law of Liberty

Because I now have received this perfect law from God, I have the same perfect law to give out to a lost soul and dying world. I have the blessed privilege to release His love and forgiveness out of me. Whenever we release that perfect law, I believe someone, somewhere, gets saved.

We can look at the example of Stephen, as told in Acts chapter 7. Stephen was stoned to death for his preaching of the gospel. I believe Stephen would have gone to heaven if he would have said, "Lord, I don't understand this. All I was doing was preaching your Word. I was doing it the best I knew how. Father, it is just not fair! Look at all those stones flying at me! I just don't understand this!" But when Stephen said, *"Lay not this sin to their charge"* (Acts 7:60), powerful energy was released from heaven. Many people were saved, including that notorious Saul (Paul), who was one of the chief persecutors of the early church...(he) became one of the great leaders of the early church. He is also credited for being the writer of the major portion of the New Testament. I believe Stephen rejoices every time someone gets saved through the writings and life of Paul in the Bible.

James 2:12 says, "S*o speak ye, and do, as they that shall be judged by the law of liberty."* Here we see that we are going to be judged by this law. If that is the case, I want to know about that law. If it is going to judge me, I must understand its principles and be able to operate it.

James 2:13 says, *"For he shall have judgment without mercy, if he hath showed no mercy; and mercy rejoiceth against judgment.*" When we extend love and mercy to wrongdoers, we are operating the perfect law of liberty.

Forgiveness is an act of your will. Temptation hits you in the realm of your feelings and thought life. You need to go past your feelings and emotions and take out the agape love of God, which is spread abroad in your heart by the Holy Spirit. If you have the Holy Spirit, you do not need to pray for more love. What you need to know is how to get the love out that you already have, and how to release the Holy Spirit in your life. It means to reach down and take out the love of God say, "Oh Father, I thank you and praise you, even though I do not feel any love for this person. I thank you Father, for your agape love that is in my heart by the Holy Spirit. I now take that love and release forgiveness for this person."

In Numbers 12, Miriam and Aaron did not respect the call of God on the life of Moses. They did not appreciate his leadership, and they criticized his wife. Moses had a real case of in-law trouble on his hands. In the time to follow, Miriam became a leper. I believe Aaron and the whole host of Israel could have interceded for Miriam's healing and she would not have been healed. But when Moses cried unto the Lord, *"Heal her now, O God, I beseech thee,"* Miriam was delivered.

The Lord showed me that there is no one on the face of the earth who can release such energy from heaven as when the person who has been hurt prays for the person who hurt them....The ministry of Jesus is a ministry of new beginnings. We need to learn how to receive our new beginning before we will be able to give one to someone else. We cannot give what we first do not possess ourselves. No longer can we box others in. We must set them free.

Forgiveness is an act of our will, not our feelings. The agape love of God that is shed abroad in our heart, must flow forth and always dispense life.

God spoke into my heart that He wanted to release me into creative living. I had to get rid of my little remembrance book and all the junk crowding my life....I began to understand the perfect law. Every time I forgive I am going to receive forgiveness. If I give mercy, I am going to receive mercy. Every time I give blessing, I am going to receive blessing. I Peter 3:9 says, "*Not rendering evil for evil, railing for railing*" that would be the wrong law in motion, "*but contrariwise blessing: knowing that ye are thereunto called, that ye should inherit a blessing.*"

Learning to Apply the Law

After the church meeting Matilda taught that weekend, the words she spoke boiled inside me. Her teaching on forgiveness and blessing was such a revelation to me. Feeling excited and apprehensive at the same time, I read her little book, *Leap for Joy*, over and over.

David acted the same when I went home. We still weren't talking. I had written his name on the red paper and mumbled forgiveness and blessing over him, crumpled the paper and thrown it in the basket as it passed. I wasn't feeling any different. I was so sad inside, so sorry I wasn't *feeling* forgiveness.

It was about noon one day the next week. I was cleaning the bathroom floor on my hands and knees by the toilet when

I was overcome with the knowledge that I really did need to *voice* my forgiveness and blessing over David in as heartfelt a way as I could. I sat there on the floor and used the porcelain throne as an altar. I began to cry out to God. I said, "Lord, You know how I feel, I don't really want to bless him, but by an act of my will, I do. I forgive him now and bless him." I raised my hands over my head and said, "Lord, I bless everything he does today. I bless the works of his hands. I bless his body, I bless..." I blessed everything I could think of. I didn't feel much. I wiped my eyes with the convenient toilet tissue and got up. I felt better that I was obedient.

Honestly, about 10 minutes later, David came home for lunch. I was just walking out of the bathroom when he walked in the front door and I was surprised to see him. He never came home for lunch. He looked depressed and even grayish in his countenance.

Something in me was different. I did not know exactly what, but I wasn't mad at him anymore.

Abruptly he said, "I don't think I love you anymore."

"Me either."

"If it weren't for the boys, I'd leave."

"Me too."

That was more words than we had spoken in weeks.

So we went in and sat down on the bed. I said, "Can I tell you something?"

He said, "Yes." Now that his big announcement was out he seemed relieved.

I began to share with him all that Matilda had taught us about forgiveness and blessing. Showing him the book, I told him I gave him a new life from that moment on and did not hold anything against him, like Jesus did on the cross. I told him that I had just done that on the bathroom floor. I had blessed him in every area I could think of. He was overcome and we both started crying. We sat there crying and holding hands. We tried to think of the reasons we were angry with each other this time and couldn't remember.

We realized our hurts, wounds and harsh words had erected a big wall between us. As we talked and cried there, I felt those walls crumble. I could almost see it in my mind.

Satan had deceived us into thinking we did not love each other and an hour later we could not believe it, because we knew we did love each other. We have never stopped.

> **James 3:16-18** For where envying and strife is, there is confusion and every evil work. [17]But the wisdom that is from above is first pure, then peaceable, gentle, and easy to be entreated, full of mercy and good fruits, without partiality, and without hypocrisy. [18]And the fruit of righteousness is sown in peace of them that make peace."

That's exactly what happened to us. We had created a space for strife to thrive and so there was a lot of confusion and evil at work in our home.

We began to recognize every time strife would rise up. We made a decision together not to allow it in our home.

Harmony the Best Way to Live

Every time David hurt me, by an act of my will I forgave and blessed him, whether I felt like it or not. I was determined that the perfect law was going to be at work in me and my family.

I took it literally. I didn't just say, "Oh, well, that's a great teaching." I began to apply everything I had learned. If I had to be the first to forgive, so be it. Someone has so be first. If it had to be me, that was fine. Sometimes we have to get over ourselves and how we feel and what we want. I had to, so I could live a blessed and peaceful life. I had to want what

God wanted more than what I wanted. It was another decision. David and I were determined not to allow strife to dominate our lives anymore.

David began to do the same thing. I did not nag him into it. It became such a revelation to both of us that we began to apply it with our children, people in stores, people on the highway, relatives. Anyone. Everyone.

I talked to my children about it a lot. It's not like they always wanted to listen, but they were there with me, doing life, so I just talked about what we were learning. I did not go into all the details of our marriage at the time.

Corey was dealing with a severe head cold one day in high school. He wasn't necessarily thrilled with all I was saying, but on this particular day, he came down to breakfast blowing his nose, frustrated that this cold had gone on so long.

Casually I asked, "Have you forgiven everybody who's hurt you?"

He got so angry! "I can't believe you would say that!"

So I just turned back to the stove and kept scrambling eggs. I wasn't really moved any more by attitudes. I knew God had to do the work. I glanced back a second later and he had bowed his head at the table. I just kept scrambling knowing he was praying. Your children hear you whether you think they do or not. Don't let their words and facial expression fool you.

The next morning every cold symptom was gone, completely. I think Corey was surprised. I really feel that when he forgave someone, it closed the door for the enemy to put sickness on him. God in turned blessed him and healed him.

Greater Blessing

I read an article in a magazine not long after we stepped into this new way of thinking—new to us anyway. It was about living in harmony. We were doing pretty well at keeping our words peaceful and forgiving and blessing. The Word says God commands a blessing when you live in unity.

> **Psalm 133**
> Behold, how good and how pleasant *it is*
> For brethren to dwell together in unity! [2] *It is*
> like the precious oil upon the head,
> Running down on the beard, The beard of
> Aaron, Running down on the edge of his
> garments. [3] *It is* like the dew of Hermon,
> Descending upon the mountains of Zion; For
> there the LORD commanded the blessing—Life
> forevermore.

After reading the article, we were even more excited. David and I were getting revelation together in these areas. It was dramatically changing our lives. It is great when two married people can walk together in unity. It was glorious...not always easy, but it was wonderful.

We walked it out day by day. We refused to allow strife to destroy our unity.

Several months later I started to get this strange feeling that there was something wrong between us. I would not keep anything in the dark anymore, so I asked David, "Is there anything wrong between us? I have this odd feeling."

He said, "No, nothing's wrong."

But I still had this nagging feeling something was wrong.

Several different days when David walked in the door from work, my stomach flipped anxiously. I would ask him again. He would said, "No, nothing's wrong. Everything is fine." Then I asked him to pray for me. He would and it would go away.

Several weeks went by and we went on a business trip to Colorado. All the way on our flight, I had that same anxious feeling. I didn't say anything because I thought I was being silly.

We got to our hotel and I couldn't stand it anymore. I knew this was not going to be a pleasant trip for me if I didn't get rid of this feeling. So I asked him again. He said, "There is absolutely nothing wrong." We knew the devil was trying to bring strife in where there was no strife, and he wasn't giving up easily.

David prayed for me again and we told the devil to leave me and our marriage alone. We took authority over our marriage. We knew victory was ours. We had already experienced it. Nothing was going to steal our peace.

That feeling left and never came back. The devil does not want husbands and wives and children to have unity. He is always trying to divide. Division happens in families, relationships, and churches all the time.

When people grab hold of the truth about unity and really believe a commanded blessing comes upon them if they walk in the truth that they know, it will change their lives. It will change families, and churches, and businesses and cities.

When I was talking to Matilda recently, she told me, "The Jesus in me should not be fighting against the Jesus in you." If people would realize that in churches, there would be no more church splits. Even if people left the church, it would be in the right way. They would be forgiving and blessing.

I believe the commanded blessing of unity found in true forgiveness is not just for married couples and children, but also for churches, organizations and businesses. If they received this truth about the Perfect Law of Liberty and walked in it, whole communities, cities and governments would change. That's a pretty lofty thought. But as we know, the Word says, *nothing* is impossible with God (Matthew 19:26)! God did it in our lives. He restored us to a place that we now help others who are struggling. It's so foreign to me now that we could have ever lived in such strife. God is the one who changes things in us by His Spirit. We have to be the guardian of our own hearts and words.

David and I have been married 41 years this year. For the last 24 years God has proven Himself faithful to His Word. As we have forgiven and blessed each other and others, we have seen great blessing.

I won't say we we've never had another stressful discussion, but we don't allow it to stay that way.

Bunny Rug Trouble

Several years ago David and I were in the mountains. It was so refreshing and peaceful. David said I could buy something before we left. I looked around for several hours and found a rug with bunnies all around the edge. I thought it was precious, but I knew it was more than I should spend. So I hinted about it all afternoon. He didn't get the hint. I thought, *Well, I just won't get anything.* I wasn't going to ask him for it; it was obvious I wanted it.

Sometimes we can be so ridiculous. I was so frustrated. I thought he should know, and he wondered what was wrong with me as we drove down the mountain and I wasn't talking. I had digressed back to the mentality of "I'll punish him; I just won't talk."

Finally I said, "I just have to tell you. I am upset because you didn't get me the bunny rug." He said, "You didn't ask for it." We talked about it a while. We got all the old junk out in the open. I forgave him, even though he didn't do anything. He was not offended at my silliness. I said, "You know, when we get home we will need to be in unity, because we are going to have a lot of phone messages of people who want us to pray for them."

So we prayed then and kind of laughed about the enemy's attempt to derail us. When we got home we had seven phone messages from people who needed prayer.

It wasn't worth being in disagreement for one minute, because we knew we would be praying over our children and others.

A friend of mine would later laugh and say, "Paige, tell us about the bunny rug controversy." The enemy can use the smallest things that don't even matter to destroy peace and unity, if we let him. A bunny rug, of all things.

Years later, we were in a meeting when a man began to prophesy over us. He said David had the gift of administration—which he does, then he said, "You two used to be tied together with barbed wire. Now you're tied together with lace."

What a beautiful verbal picture of God's work in our lives. He truly is our very present help in trouble (Psalm 46:1).

When our son Brice got married, I looked up at the altar. There were David and Corey standing with Brice. Weddings are always touching and beautiful, especially your children's. I started to cry. I wasn't crying because Brice looked so handsome and all my men were so happy. I was crying because I thought, *If I had divorced years ago, what would this day look like?* I was overwhelmed with thankfulness to God. He has shown us the truth and helped us walk in it. He had saved our family, and now we help others.

As the prophet Nahum said,

Nahum 1:7 AMP The Lord is good, a Strength *and* Stronghold in the day of trouble; He knows (recognizes, has knowledge of, and understands) those who take refuge *and* trust in Him.

Psalm 22:3 KJV

But thou art holy, O thou that inhabitest
the praises of Israel.

12

COME INTO HIS GATES WITH THANKSGIVING, INTO HIS COURTS WITH PRAISE

The light streaming through the window illuminated the verses I was reading. I had read these scripture passages many times but now became absorbed in them for several minutes. I read them over and over. I almost forgot I was substituting in a junior high classroom.

Suddenly I realized I had been living out these scriptures and didn't even know it.

> **Philippians 4:6-7** Be anxious for nothing, but in everything by prayer and supplication, with thanksgiving, let your requests be made known to God; [7] and the peace of God, which surpasses all understanding, will guard your hearts and minds through Christ Jesus.

> **Colossians 4:2** Continue earnestly in prayer, being vigilant in it with thanksgiving

These scriptures had been a key to answered prayer in my life and in the lives of others. There are many scriptures on prayer in the Word.

> **James 5:16b** …the effective, fervent prayer of a righteous man avails much.

> **Matthew 21:21** And whatever things you ask in prayer, believing, you will receive."

> **I Thessalonians 5:17** pray without ceasing,

> **Hebrews 11:6b** …for he who comes to God must believe that He is, and *that* He is a rewarder of those who diligently seek Him

There are many men and women spoken of in the Bible who lived lives of prayer. Abraham was known as a "friend of God." David prayed and worshipped as he tended sheep in the hills. He became a mighty man of God and king of all Israel. Daniel prayed in captivity and saw God's hand move and the lions' mouths shut. All the apostles became men of prayer. Jesus was certainly a man of prayer, and he was the greatest teacher on prayer. When the disciples asked Him how to pray, He said, "Pray like this, 'Father, which art in heaven, hallowed be thy name." (Matthew 9:6-13 records the complete prayer). Many of us grew up learning the Lord's Prayer.

I have studied these scriptures above and more about prayer. I wondered what it meant in Luke 18:1 to "always pray and faint not." Many times in my life I've prayed, as most do, even fervently, but the circumstances seemed so gigantic. When I would get up from praying, I just picked the burdens or worry back up like a sack of potatoes and carried it along with me again. I should have left the burdens where I took them in the first place, with Jesus.

We drag our requests around behind us like luggage and pray again, hoping our burden will be lifted and hoping God will answer soon.

Years ago, I heard a story about a pastor whose daughter had started taking drugs and left home. The pastor prayed and cried out to God for her life for several years. He saw no change.

One day when he was crying out, again, God said to him, "If you will quit crying and whining to Me and start praising Me and thanking Me, I will bring her back." So, just as God instructed, this pastor began to thank God and praise Him that his daughter would be set free and that she was coming home.

A year and a half later he was a visiting preacher in a church and sitting on the platform when he saw his daughter walk into the back of the church. She came up to the front and gave her life to the Lord. She is still serving God today.

Kenneth Hagin told a story about a pastor who preached in many churches and traveled a lot. He was diagnosed with tuberculosis. In every church where he preached after being diagnosed, he asked the people to pray that he would be healed. They all agreed that they would. Years later, he was lying on his bed and the doctors said he didn't have long to live.

He was very weak, couldn't walk and could barely speak. His family left the house for a short time. He was alone. He said to himself, "Well, if God was going to heal me because of all those prayers, I would be healed. So I guess I'll just praise God anyway."

So he crawled out of the house because he was so weak and ended up crawling under some bushes in the yard. He whispered as loud as he could, "I praise you, God."

It sounded like a raspy whisper. But he kept speaking his

praise and thanks. An hour later, he was standing next to those bushes shouting his praise, with his arms in the air. He had been totally healed!

Power Twins

I've heard people refer to thanksgiving and praise as the power twins. When you are thanking God and praising Him despite your circumstances, it is hard to stay in doubt and unbelief.

Even if you don't believe when you start to lay your requests before God and begin thanking Him and praising Him, as you continue, your faith rises. Think of it like a spiritual thermometer with rising mercury. When you praise God and thank Him, the low areas of doubt and unbelief in your heart begin to rise to faith in God.

> **I John 5:4b** And this is the victory that has overcome the world—our faith.

When doubt tries to come back and gain ground in your heart and mind again, begin praising and thanking God again. The Holy Spirit will do a deep work in you as you do. Stand on the Word, speak it forth and praise God for the outcome. The *outcome* is the promise God made to you in His Word, whether it is wholeness in your body or full storehouses in your finances or a prodigal returning to the Father.

That day in the classroom as I looked at the scriptures in Colossians and Philippians, I realized that I had been following their instruction for 11 years, without even knowing it.

The Lord healed me and revealed that His Word was "life to my bones and health to me" from Proverbs 4:20-22. My marriage was restored. I was using this principle of praise and thanksgiving in every area of my life. I prayed this way for our children and our finances.

I saw great fruit from these years of praying, thanking God for His answer and praising Him that He had answered my prayers before I saw it in the natural. I also praise and thank Him after I see it. Then I rejoice!

I have been healed. One of my sons has been healed. David's job is prospering. Our marriage is in unity. Our children are hungering and thirsting after righteousness and serving God.

Whenever I see an area I need to pray about, I find a scripture, or more than one, that covers that problem. Using an example of fear, I would pray something like this: "Lord, Your Word says I do 'not have a spirit of fear, but of power, love and a sound mind.' So that's what I say. I say, what You say, Lord. Fear, you leave me alone in Jesus' name. I don't own fear. It's not mine. I thank You, Lord that I have a sound mind and I do not fear."

I just say and pray what God says about me. That's His will. I put His Word in my mouth and I speak it back to Him. Then I praise and thank Him. I might do it ten or more times to get my heart and mind in agreement with God's Word that I am speaking.

The other day, my three-year old granddaughter was singing. I was trying to hear her words. She was a few feet away from me and her hand was over her heart while she swayed back and forth. I said, "What is that you're singing?" She looked over her shoulder at me like it was a private moment. I asked again, "What song is it?"

She said, "Oh, it's a song in my heart to the Lord. I got it at the store and I put it in my mouth."

That's exactly what we do. We take His Word—that is God Himself according to John 1:1—and put it in our hearts and mouths.

Matthew 12:34 For out of the abundance of the heart the mouth speaks.

Luke 6:45 For out of the abundance of the heart his mouth speaks.

The words we speak are powerful. Even at the point a person receives Jesus as his Savior, the Bible says to confess with your mouth that Jesus is your Lord (Romans 10:9).

There are some Christians who have been saved 30, 40 or even 50 years who need the Word to be life to them and their source of perspective instead of their current circumstances. I have heard Christians pray for a job and get up and say, "I hope I get one." Instead of that old way of speaking, "when you pray, believe that He is and He is the rewarder of those who diligently seek Him" (Hebrews 11:6b).

God Inhabits the Praises of His People

David says in Psalm 22:3 (KJV) "God inhabits the praises of Israel" (His people). When we inhabit a place, we go in and live there. We put our furniture in place. We get in our comfy chair with our fuzzy socks and make it home.

Since "God inhabits the praises of His people" He wants to come in and sit with you and speak to you, to be close to you.

He sees you when you are brokenhearted, he doesn't run when you are weary. He's there. He's just waiting for His children to have an attitude of faith and praise.

He sees all the negative things going on in the world, of course, He's God. He meets people where they are. He knows how many hairs are on your head (Matthew 10:30). Yet He loves it when we praise Him in the midst of trouble. Like

David. Like Joseph. Like Daniel.

God's heart says, "Praise Me when your boat is sinking in a storm, see if I won't rescue you. Praise Me when you are in chains and see if I won't free you. Praise me when you have no food and see if I won't multiply it. Praise me when there is sickness and see if I won't raise up that person you love. See if I won't prosper you. See if I won't meet every need you have according to My riches in glory. Praise Me so I can linger with you."

Years ago, I saw the movie *Pollyanna*. You've probably seen it too. It's about a little girl who goes to live with her rich aunt. Her parents had been missionaries and she had always been poor. Her aunt is always negative, the servants are grouchy, and the townspeople are the same.

Pollyanna is a sweet child who sees good in everything, and she talks to everyone about the "Glad Game" she and her father played. Her father taught her how to be thankful. Even when negative things happened in her life, she could find something to be glad about.

The people of the town and her aunt made light of her "glad talk." One even asks, "What's all this glad about this, glad about that?" The pastor even preached fire and brimstone every Sunday, so loud the light fixtures shook and people went home with upset stomachs.

Gradually Pollyanna made friendships around town and was so thankful and glad about everything that the people started to change. They were happier and life seemed brighter, except for Sundays.

One day Pollyanna came across the pastor on a hill practicing his fire and brimstone sermon. After listening for a while, she innocently told him that her dad used to preach that way until he discovered the "glad passages." He called them the "happy texts." There are 826 happy texts in the Bible. Like "Rejoice always" (Philippians 4:4).

You see this pastor was miserable. He wasn't really

looking at who God was. He was looking at all the negative things in life, so that's how he preached. He wanted "to get the sin out of the people." But that's why everyone hated Sundays and had stomach aches. There was no joy, thankfulness or love in his sermons.

When he realized what he had done to himself and the townspeople, he repented and promised to change. The people began to hope again. The whole town changed because of one little girl's thankfulness. They renamed the town Glad Town.

I realize this is fiction, but God can teach us through anything. This story impressed upon me that thankfulness and a glad heart changes people and situations.

God wants us all to live, not in a what-will-be world, but in your own world, with the Word of God, the promises of God and with thanksgiving and praise on our lips. Why not? I believe He is waiting for His people to believe Him, to take His Word and behave like it is true, to praise Him in the midst of life—good or difficult—to prove Him as He says to do in scripture.

> **Malachi 3:10 KJV** Bring ye all the tithes into the storehouse, that there may be meat in mine house, and prove me now herewith, saith the LORD of hosts, if I will not open you the windows of heaven, and pour you out a blessing, that there shall not be room enough to receive it.

He tells us He wants to prove Himself to us, that He will do what He says He will do! In Luke 1:37b it even says, "For with God nothing will be impossible."

There is an old hymn "Trust Me and Try Me" by Lydia Shivers Leech, composed in 1873 based on this verse about God wanting to prove Himself to us, if we will just ask.

We say it and we sing it, we should also expect it!

Sometimes the answer to our prayers can come in minutes, or it could take years. He is not an automated, push button God. He is a God that sets things right and in order. He is working to bring about the best for us.

> **Psalm 68:19 KJV** Blessed *be* the Lord, *Who* daily loads us *with benefits,* The God of our salvation! Selah

> **Jeremiah 29:11** For I know the thoughts that I think toward you, says the LORD, thoughts of peace and not of evil, to give you a future and a hope.

Sometimes, we, His children, bought by the blood of Jesus, His own Son, act like the problem we have is too hard for the Almighty. We think this sickness might be too tough for the blood of Jesus to heal. This prodigal son might be too far away and hardened for the Good Shepherd Who goes after the one to bring him to safety. This one's sin is so deep, even God who created all things can't pull him out, can't change him, can't deliver him forever.

We would never voice those sentiments out loud, but in the midst of our crying out in prayer we might feel it. It manifests in those lingering hopeless feelings when we get up from our knees and walk away. If we continue to pray and live that way as Christians, what good is it to anyone? There is nothing but disappointment and discouragement in life, and all because we might have to *wait* to see God's answer.

What would happen in your life if after you've prayed and believed and not seen results right away, you begin to speak the Word and praise God for the answer to your financial, marital, physical, and spiritual problems? Praise Him because He has an answer. Praise Him because He is good. Praise Him that He has made you an overcomer!

Every promise in the Word is yours. Take the promises, the Word, and put it in your heart and mouth. Keep your confession lined up with the truth.

There is a hymn based on Matthew 19:26 which says "but with God all things are possible."

> Only believe, only believe,
> All things are possible,
> Only believe.[1]

I encourage you to write down your smallest and your most difficult prayer requests. Do it like I did in the first chapter if you want to, hold them up to God. Find a scripture that covers your problem. Say to the Lord, the One Who loves you the most, "This is what you say, Father, about my son, daughter, family, wife, etc. So I say what You say, from now on."

I leave you with these scriptures. They resonate loudly in my ears and heart when I get impatient to see God's hand moving faster.

Hebrews 10:35-38 Therefore do not cast away your confidence, which has great reward. [36] For you have need of endurance, so that after you have done the will of God, you may receive the promise: [37] "For yet a little while, *And* He who is coming will come and will not tarry. [38] Now the just shall live by faith; But if *anyone* draws back, My soul has no pleasure in him."

Hebrews 11:1 Now faith is the substance of things hoped for, the evidence of things not seen.

---

[1] By Paul Rader ©1921, owned by Mary C. Rader ©1949 renewed.

Blessings to you! May your faith in God rise to greater heights than you've even imagined.

I pray for each one of you now, as I've prayed for myself, my family and others:

I pray, Lord, that they will be enlightened by the Holy Spirit. That they will have the peace of God and know the depths, breadths, and heights of the Father's love. That their faith will be so strengthened that no turmoil, wind of doctrine, opinions of men, fear, or physical pain will deceive them into doubt and unbelief. I pray, Lord, that they will say "yes" to everything You say about them! You say Lord, when they are saved that You take them out of the kingdom of darkness and set them in the kingdom of your dear Son. You say, Lord, they are blessed to be a blessing, they are healed, set free, and made whole. You say, Lord, they have the mind of Christ, they are seated right now in heavenly places, in the spirit, in Jesus Christ. They are joint heirs with Jesus, and He is their righteousness forever. I pray Lord that they say "yes."

I thank you Lord, that they will be vigilant to keep their hearts and minds stayed on the Word and only speak the truths in the Word, no matter what they are going through. I thank you, Lord, You are their teacher by Your spirit and they are overcomers in this life.

I thank you, Lord, they will begin to get the Word so deep in their hearts. They will decree a thing, as it says in Job 22:28, and it will be established for them, according to the Word, in Jesus' name.

I bless you now. May you know how lovely and precious you are to the Father who created all things. How He delights in you. His thoughts are always toward you. His plans for you are good forever. His love never fails!

–Paige Jackson

Available on Amazon

Contact the author at
paigejacksoncloud9@gmail.com

Made in the USA
Columbia, SC
06 November 2017